Prefaces to SHAKESPEARE

Harley Granville-Barker

Othello

B. T. BATSFORD LTD
LONDON

FIRST PUBLISHED 1930
FIRST PUBLISHED IN THIS EDITION 1982

PRINTED IN GREAT BRITAIN
BY BILLING AND SONS LTD, GUILDFORD, LONDON AND WORCESTER
FOR THE PUBLISHERS
B. T. BATSFORD LTD
4 FITZHARDINGE STREET, LONDON W1H 0AH

ISBN 0 7134 4326 X

FOREWORD
by Sir John Gielgud

A NUMBER of older players used to describe Harley Granville-Barker to me very vividly as he was when they had worked with him before the 1914–18 War.

He had been slim and poetic-looking in those days, a vegetarian like his close friend and mentor Bernard Shaw. Wearing sandals and chewing nuts, infinitely demanding as he was when directing Shakespeare, they strove to please him in his striving for perfection, and were lost in admiration of his innovations—an almost uncut text, only two intervals and a simple stylized decor, with a builtout forestage, no footlights, and a breakneck speed in delivery from his cast. On first nights he would pin last minute notes of exhortation on their dressing-room mirrors: 'Be swift, be swift, be not poetical' (to Cathleen Nesbitt as Perdita).

When I first caught sight of him myself in 1928 he looked impressive enough, but more like a successful businessman. He was beginning to put on weight, and wore a dark suit and a Homburg hat. But I was instantly to become aware of his sureness and authority. Even though his wife (watching jealously from the darkness of the dress circle), interrupted him once or twice with a firm 'Harley! lunch . . .' to which, alas, he obediently complied, he had contrived in two short hours to redirect (and even in one of the plays recast the leading part) with unerring and unimpeachable finality.

Though he lived for a time in England, he soon became dissatisfied with trying to become a country squire and moved to Paris. Here he wrote the Shakespeare *Prefaces* and lectured at the Sorbonne. In 1937–8, when he came to see some Shakespearean productions of mine, he wrote me a number of brilliant letters of criticism which I had the good sense to keep. And in 1939, when I was to take *Hamlet* to Elsinore, after a preliminary week at the Lyceum, I heard he was in London and wrote begging him to come to a late rehearsal. Next morning he summoned me to the Ritz, and gave me three hours of invaluable and detailed notes with which I was able to improve my own performance and that of my company.

Finally, in 1940, Lewis Casson and Tyrone Guthrie prevailed on him to help us in a production of *King Lear* at the Old Vic. He stayed at the Athenaeum and for ten days we had him to ourselves. Of those ten days of rehearsals at the Vic I have written some account elsewhere. Even the Fall of France, which was to appal us some weeks later, could not make me forget the magic excitement of working under Barker for those few short days—the agonising struggles to satisfy his demands, the devastating accuracy of his strictures, the enormous satisfaction of earning an occasional note of approval. Then, just after the first dress rehearsal, he was gone, though during the subsequent weeks he would still write me post-cards mentioning points which he had reconsidered and things that he had meant to say.

In 1945 I was playing Hamlet again for the last time and heard he had been to see a matinée. Rather timidly I invited him and his wife to dine with me at my house on the very night when Peace was to be declared. But I found him considerably aged and silent and did not press him to talk about the theatre before his wife. After dinner, however, he did draw me aside and said some kind things about my performance. A few days later he wrote me a last letter, apologising for not having remembered the 1939 production and the help he had given me in improving it.

The following year he died in Paris, but though with a few of his staunchest admirers, I begged to be allowed to organise a Memorial Service, Mrs Barker sent strict injunctions that she had no wish for him to be publicly commemorated 'by actors' and we were forced to abandon the idea. I can hardly believe that Barker would have approved her decision. Though he plainly despised the commercial trappings of our profession—its gossip, intrigue and jealousy, its publicity, cheapness and ephemeral glories and disasters—I cannot but think of him as a great master, the nearest theatrical equivalent to Toscanini among the many brilliant colleagues I have been fortunate to work with during my long career.

July 1981

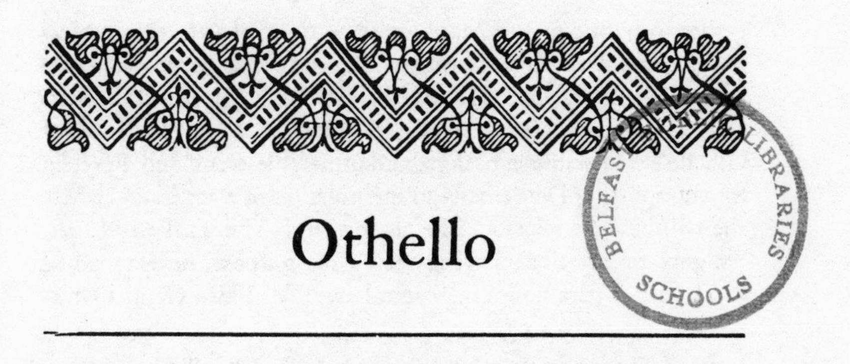

Othello

Shakespeare, as his habit was, took a ready-made story to work upon. It is as if, for a start, he feels a need to tie his exuberant imagination to something he can rank as fact. Cinthio's is a convincing story; its characters are clearly drawn, and it is, in its spare fashion, very well told. There was much to attract him in it: the romantic setting in Venice and Cyprus (he has never cared for commonplace backgrounds); the exotic figure of the Moor (of rarer stuff than Shylock), and the "Machiavellian" Ensign. It deals, moreover, with the degradation of love between man and woman, a subject in which about this time he was finding varied material, both for tragedy and for such so-called comedies as *Troilus and Cressida* and *Measure for Measure*. The story itself he by no means improves in the course of compressing it into drama; he omits, indeed, some of its most striking touches, and, towards its crux, so jeopardizes its very credibility that all his craftsman's skill is needed to save this from collapse. But he endows Cinthio's outlined characters with an extraordinary actuality and vitality; Desdemona and Emilia, Othello himself, Iago, Cassio, Roderigo and Bianca making a group in this respect unrivaled in the rest of his work. And he charges the sordid matter of his original with poetry to make it the high tragedy we know.

The Story and the Play

He makes changes he could have avoided, but the purpose of them is clear. In the story Desdemona and the Moor—although she has married him against her parents' wish—have lived together in harmony and peace for some time. Shakespeare prefers an elopement for his starting point, since this gives an initial impetus to the action. He invents also the Cyprus war and its sudden crisis. Here is increased impetus, some evidence of Othello's soldiership, a background of notable event, and a pretext for transporting Desdemona to the isolation of a far island where she will be defenseless and he all-powerful. The Turks and their "mighty preparation" having served his purpose, he gets rid of them with a (dramatically) cynical ease. A "Third Gentleman's"

> News, lords! our wars are done.
> The desperate tempest hath so banged the Turks,
> That their designment halts. . . .

with Othello's as summary

> News, friends; our wars are done. The Turks are drowned. . . .

suffice. But it is not simply that he has no further use for them. They would be a positive hindrance to him now. For Iago must be set to work without more delay, and an Othello braced to action might prove intractable material. Jealousy thrives best in a stagnant soil.

The initial elopement must not be allowed to suggest a second tragedy of "violent delights" leading to "violent ends," for we are to have no such show of youthful folly. To prevent this the characters of Othello and Desdemona themselves are firmly outlined from the first; his austere dignity; the calm with which—mere girl that she is!—she faces the majestic Senate, confutes her father and wins her cause. And while Shakespeare cannot, without unduly slackening the play's action, produce the effect of the harmony and tranquillity of life in which the story discovers them, to replace this he sends them separately to Cyprus and, after bare escape with their lives—from the very tempest that so bangs the Turks, thus put to double use—reunites them in such an ecstasy of happiness that, cries Othello,

> I fear,
> My soul hath her content so absolute,
> That not another comfort like to this
> Succeeds in unknown fate.

Among other changes, the Captain's wife disappears.[1] Three wives would be one too many. In her place—conjured out of a single phrase in the story concerning a courtesan he was about to visit—we have Bianca, whose frailty, with its affectations of virtue, is set both against Desdemona's innate chastity and Emilia's coarser honesty, the play's pattern of womanhood being thus varied and enlarged. And Bianca is put to appropriate use in the scene in which Othello, eavesdropping, takes what he hears of Cassio's light talk of her for further proof of Desdemona's guilt.

In the story the Ensign's wife ("a young, fair and virtuous lady; and being of Italian birth, she was much loved by Desdemona, who spent the greater part of every day with her"[2]) knows what is going forward, refuses all share in it, but dare not speak out for fear of him. For a combination of reasons Shakespeare cannot accept this. Such a theme demands elaboration and, elaborated, might prove engrossing, making the minor character the more interesting of the two. Nor could he well place an immobilized Emilia of this quality beside the passive Desdemona; he needs contrast here, not likeness. So he retains the intimacy, but changes the nature of it, makes them waiting-woman and mistress, and in every way contrasts them.[3] He contrasts his Emilia with Iago also; the growth of her loyal affection with his frigid treachery, her blindness to what is passing with his sharp wit.

To this end the episode of the handkerchief, as the story has it, is reshaped. The happy trait of the "*eccelentimente di mano,*" which lets the wicked Ensign himself filch the handkerchief from

[1] The Furness Variorum gives us five pages of footnotes upon Iago's description of Cassio in the first scene of the play as

a Florentine,
A fellow almost damned in a fair wife . . .

in face of the fact that Cassio, as it turns out, has no wife. But the explanation is surely simple enough. Shakespeare, when he wrote the line, meant to follow the story in this respect. Later, for good reasons, he changed his mind and gave Bianca to Cassio for a mistress instead, omitting, however, to alter the text of this first scene. And Cassio was "almost damned" because every fellow with a fair wife is, in Iago's estimation, a predestined cuckold.

[2] I quote, here and elsewhere, from the translation in the Furness Variorum.

[3] But Emilia is a waiting-gentlewoman. No rigid class-distinction is involved.

Desdemona's girdle, is sacrificed. Iago, instead, has, says Emilia,

> a hundred times
> Wooed me to steal it . . .

and, having at last picked it up, she gives it him and adds a covering lie to the fault. No more than this is left of the silent complicity of the story, though enough even so—coarse-grained as she is made, and for all Shakespeare's own dramatic "*eccelentimente di mano*"—to do some damage to Emilia's credit with us. The episode now serves as one more illustration of Iago's talent for using other hands to do his work for him. Roderigo, Cassio, Emilia, Bianca too; when he is in the vein they are his cat's-paws all. Not until, his affairs going awry, he gives Cassio that sword-slash in the dark, does he, we may remark, *do* one single thing himself. And even this, and even the subsequent stabbing of Roderigo, as will later appear, he bungles.

Again, the Captain in the story knows that the handkerchief he finds in his room is Desdemona's, and he attempts to return it to her; and, later, his wife is seen by the Moor at her window copying its embroidery, even as Bianca is asked to copy it. This goes well enough in a story. But clearly Cassio cannot be allowed to know. The play's close-knit action and its generalizing of location will make access to Desdemona seem easy, and his respect for her would never let him knowingly give her handkerchief to Bianca.

The Ensign's little daughter, whom Desdemona loves, is omitted. Iago as a fond father! Did Shakespeare feel that such a gem of irony might outshine the rest?

Roderigo is Shakespeare's invention. His gulling provides the shadow of an underplot, some comic relief—he makes a ridiculous counterpart to the nobler victim—and something more dramatically valuable than either. For, colorless himself, he is the mirror in which can be reflected an Iago that the stress of the main action will hardly let us see; cynically at his ease, ostentatiously base, yet meretricious even in this, and reckless too. Cinthio's Ensign—drawn like the rest in outline only, but firmly and precisely, without one false stroke—is patient, single-minded, veritably austere in his wickedness, and is victorious to the last, another story being needed to give him his deserts. But Iago must come by his within the compass of the play. And, for all his destructive cunning, here, from the beginning, is his own destruction implicit; in the cankering vanity, the innate malignity, crass appetite and mere itch to do evil, so vaingloriously displayed. It is in his coarse contempt for the "sick fool Roderigo" that his own fatal folly is visible from the first, and the more rapidly ripens.

The capital change, however, is that which converts the anonymous Moor into Othello, for with this it is that the whole brutal story is raised to the heights of tragedy. But, for all the gain, some loss is still involved. What, as Cinthio has it, could be better of its kind, after "the wicked Ensign" has resolved to wait patiently "until time and circumstance should open a path for him to engage in his foul project," than its unwitting opening by the Moor himself, who seeks and again and again questions the deprecatory villain, and waits in torture for the disclosure "which was to make him miserable to the end of his days," or than—while he is still convinced of her guilt—his demented grief for the murdered Desdemona and slowly gathering hatred of the man he had employed to murder her? But those lagging agonies, made so significant in the story—where also the very sparseness of the telling of them sets our imagination to work to fill the gaps—would provide too slack a mechanism altogether for Shakespeare's theater, with its primary need (in his eyes) for continuing and continuous action.

Ay, that's the way;
Dull not device by coldness and delay.

says Iago, when he has at last worked out his plan. And it is very much as if Shakespeare, with these dramatic drawbacks to the story in mind, were telling himself the same thing.

There is yet another capital difference between story and play. The story lacks all conflict. Cinthio's Moor is an ignorant, and—despite his bursts of rage—an unresisting victim throughout. The ignorance must be retained, or the plot, Iago's and the play's too, will collapse. Othello must be

tenderly led by the nose
As asses are.

By what replace, then, the conflict which in some sort seemingly all drama demands? Shakespeare gives us, between Iago and

Othello—as between Moor and Ensign Cinthio does not—and emphasizes from the first, radical and acute contrast of circumstance and character. In everything the two are opposed. Iago is a nobody and has his way to make, has an abundant conceit of himself and smarts under neglect; there, indeed, is the immediate spring of his villainy. Othello—while Cinthio's Moor was simply "*molto valoroso . . . per essere pio della persona*"—is of royal descent, although he has had the tactful modesty to conceal this so far from republican Venice. Again, while Desdemona in the story says to her husband, ". . . you Moors are of so hot a nature that every little trifle moves you to anger and revenge," Shakespeare gives us an Othello calm beneath Brabantio's threats and abuse, in the matter of Cassio's brawl of iron self-control, and against that he sets the gadfly Iago, impatient from the first to be stinging.[4]

The play is half through before the sting is planted, and the two characters have been developed meanwhile in no very close relation to each other. But when this becomes intimate, the contrast between them is progressively heightened until a species of conflict is created, not of action, since the story forbids that, but of the very essence of the men. And as this is distilled before us, ever more intensely—can two such elements in humanity, we are brought to asking, so opposed, peaceably partake for long one share of the world together? Is not conflict, victory and defeat innate and inevitable in what they *are*? For

> He has a daily beauty in his life
> That makes me ugly. . . .

That Iago says this, not of Othello, but of Cassio, says it incidentally, and that it somewhat belies, moreover, his diabolonian boastings, makes it none the less, but rather the more revealing. For of such intrinsic truths about themselves the most self-conscious men—and among these is Iago—will be the least

[4] One of the most remarkable things about Salvini's Othello—so I was told by William Poel, who saw and studied it—was the restraint in which he held himself until Iago's poison had begun to work in him. It made one think, said Poel, of a sleeping volcano. And when at last—and not till the play was half over—the passionate force in the man did begin to stir, the effect was terrific.

aware. Out they slip to pass unnoticed. And here is a better reason for his hatred of Othello—as we see it in action; and what Iago does is ever better evidence of the man than what he says—than all the vaunted "reasons" his intellectual vanity sets him seeking. His task demands a force beyond his braggart "wit." He finds this in the loosing of some need of his very being to reduce the nobility confronting him to baseness. He must, so instinct tells him, if he himself is to survive. Within a set arena great goodness and great wickedness cannot coexist for long; one must yield to the other, or the bounds of the arena be broken. There can be no compromise. Shakespeare gives us, then, in place of conflict of action, this conflict of being. The fortress of good, to which siege is laid, is defenselessly unaware of its own goodness, as true goodness is. We watch it falling, stone by stone.

But nobility must be brought even lower than the baseness which attacks it, if the triumph of evil is to be complete; and this dictates the culminating change from story to play. The Moor of the story stands callously by while the Ensign clubs Desdemona to death. That is horrible. But Othello is made to fall from his ideal heights to deeper damnation still, and to do the deed himself. How is this possible? Shakespeare sets himself the task—to which Iago's task inheres—of showing us, and convincingly, the process of the spiritual self-destruction which can make him capable of such a deed, to which his physical self-destruction after is the mere sequel. For, like all great tragedies, it is a tragedy of character. And it is epitomized at the end in the mockery of that one terrible paradox,

> O, thou Othello, that wert once so good, . . .
> What shall be said to thee?

That wert once so *good*!

> Why, anything;
> An honourable murderer, if you will. . . .

An honorable murderer! The soldier Othello saying it of himself. That was not within Cinthio's range.

The Shaping of the Play

It has been often enough remarked that in the action of Othello there is, for Shakespeare, an unusually near approach to classic unity.[5] "Had the scene opened in Cyprus," says Johnson, "and the preceding incidents been occasionally related, there had been little wanting to a drama of the most exact and scrupulous regularity." But this (with due respect to Johnson) makes a misleading approach. There is no aiming at regularity and falling short of it. What unity there is—and it is very defective—is simply the outcome of an economy of treatment peculiar to the needs of the play. Unity of theme, that we have. As to unity of place; this is vaguely and implicitly established for several successive scenes within the bounds of Othello's residence. But Bianca and Roderigo—Bianca particularly—are most unlikely intruders there, where a while before Othello and Desdemona have been domestically disputing over the loss of the handkerchief. And time is given no unity of treatment at all; it is contracted and expanded like a concertina. For the play's opening and closing the time of the action is the time of its acting; and such an extent of "natural" time (so to call it) is unusual. But minutes stand for hours over the sighting, docking and discharging—with a storm raging, too!—of the three ships which have carried the characters to Cyprus; the entire night of Cassio's undoing passes uninterruptedly in the speaking space of four hundred lines: and we have, of course, Othello murdering Desdemona within twenty-four hours of the consummation of their marriage, when, if Shakespeare let us—or let Othello himself—pause to consider, she plainly *cannot* be guilty of adultery.[6]

Freedom with time is, of course, one of the recognized freedoms of Shakespeare's stage; he needs only to give his exercise of it the slightest dash of plausibility. But in the maturity of his art he learns how to draw dramatic profit from it. For this play's beginning he does not, as we have noted, contract time at all. Moreover, he allows seven hundred lines to the three first scenes

[5] *The Tempest*, however, makes a nearer one.

[6] Other explanations have been offered: one, that Othello is driven to suspect Desdemona of fornication with Cassio before her marriage. But this is frivolous.

when he could well have done their business in half the space or less, could even, as Johnson suggests, have left it to be "occasionally related" afterwards. The profit is made evident when later, by contrast, we find him using contraction of time, and the heightening of tension so facilitated, to disguise the incongruities of the action. He can do this more easily if he has already familiarized us with the play's characters. And he has done that more easily by presenting them to us in the unconstraint of uncontracted time, asking us for no special effort of make-believe. Accepting what they are, we shall the more readily accept what they do. It was well, in particular, to make Iago familiarly lifelike. If his victims are to believe in him, so, in another sense, must we. Hence the profuse self-display to Roderigo. That there is as much lying as truth in it is no matter. A man's lying, once we detect it, is as eloquent of him as the truth.

The contraction of time for the arrival in Cyprus has its profitable dramatic purpose too. Shakespeare could have relegated the business to hearsay. But the spectacular excitement, the suspense, the ecstatic happiness of the reuniting of Othello and Desdemona, give the action fresh stimulus and impetus and compensate for the break in it occasioned by the voyage. Yet there must be no dwelling upon this, which is still only prelude to the capital events to come. For the same reason, the entire night of Cassio's undoing passes with the uninterrupted speaking of four hundred lines. It is no more than a sample of Iago's skill, so it must not be lingered upon either. Amid the distracting variety of its comings and goings we do not remark the contraction. As Iago himself is let suggest to us:

> Pleasure and action make the hours seem short.

Then, upon the entrance of Cassio with his propitiatory *aubade*, commences the sustained main stretch of the action, set to something more complex than a merely contracted, to a sort of ambiguous scheme of time, which is not only a profitable, but here, for Shakespeare turning story into play, an almost necessary device.[7] After which we have the long last scene set to "natural"

[7] To be examined more closely. See p. 24ff.

time, the play thus ending as it began. The swift-moving, close-packed action, fit product of Iago's ravening will, is over.

Enter Othello, and Desdemona in her bed.

—and, the dreadful deed done, all is done. And while the rest come and go about him:

Here is my journey's end. . . .

he says, at a standstill, and as in a very void of time. And as the "natural" time at the play's beginning let us learn the better what he was, so relaxation to it now lets us mark the more fully the wreck that remains.

THE SCENES IN VENICE

The three opening scenes move to a scheme of their own, in narrative and in the presentation of character. The first gives us a view of Iago which, if to be proved superficial, is yet a true one (for Shakespeare will never introduce a character misleadingly) and a sample of his double-dealing. Roderigo at the same time paints us a thick-lipped, lascivious Moor, which we discover in the second scene, with a slight stimulating shock of surprise at the sight of Othello himself, to have been merely a figment of his own jealous chagrin. There also we find quite another Iago: the modest, devoted, disciplined soldier, who, though in the trade of war he has slain men, holds it "very stuff o' the conscience to do no contrived murder," and "lacks iniquity" to do himself service. The third scene takes us to the Senate House, where Brabantio and his griefs, which have shrilly dominated the action so far, find weightier competition in the question of the war, and the State's need of Othello, whose heroic aspect is heightened by this. His dignity is next matched, in another kind, with Desdemona's. And again we receive that slight shock of surprise—so stimulating to our interest in a character—when the

maiden never bold;
Of spirit so still and quiet that her motion
Blushed at herself . . .

of Brabantio's piteous pleading proves, for all that, to be as resolute and unafraid. Here is the twinned, confident nobility which is to be brought low. And Iago, conspicuously silent throughout the scene (Othello's orders to him at its beginning and end make both him and his silence conspicuous), surveys the two, and may seem to be sizing up his task—which, a moment later, with the sniveling Roderigo for listener, he begins by re-sliming them with the foulness of his mind, as a snake will with its slime the prey to be swallowed.

The scenic mobility of Shakespeare's stage permits him up to this point to translate his narrative straightforwardly into action. We pass, that is to say, from Brabantio's house, which Desdemona has just quitted, to the Sagittary, where she and Othello are to be found, and from there to the Senate House, to which he and she (later) and Brabantio are summoned. And the movement itself is given dramatic value—by its quickening or slackening or abrupt arrest. We have the feverish impetus of Brabantio's torchlight pursuit; Othello's calm talk to Iago set in sequence and contrast to it; its encounter with the other current of the servants of the Duke upon their errand; the halt, the averted conflict; then the passing-on together of the two parties, in sobered but still hostile detachment, towards the Senate House.

Note also that such narrative as is needed of what has passed before the play begins is mainly postponed to the third of these opening scenes. By then we should be interested in the characters, and the more, therefore, in the narrative itself, which is, besides, given a dramatic value of its own by being framed as a cause pleaded before the Senate. Further, even while we listen to the rebutting of Brabantio's accusation of witchcraft by Othello's "round unvarnished tale" we shall be expecting Desdemona's appearance, the one important figure in this part of the story still to be seen. And this expectancy offsets the risk of the slackening of tension which reminiscent narrative must always involve.[8]

THE ARRIVAL IN CYPRUS

Shakespeare now breaks the continuity of the action: and such a clean break as this is with him unusual. He has to transport his characters to Cyprus. The next scene takes place there. An un-

[8] Emilia—who is *not*, as stage usage will have it, among Desdemona's attendants; why should she be?—only acquires importance much later.

measured interval of time is suggested, and no scene on shipboard or the like has been provided for a link, nor are any of the events of the voyage recounted. The tempest which drowns the Turks, and rids him of his now superfluous war, and has more thrillingly come near besides to drowning the separated Othello and Desdemona—something of this he does contrive to present to us; and we are plunged into it as we were into the crisis of the play's opening:

> What from the cape can you discern at sea?
> Nothing at all. It is a high-wrought flood;
> I cannot, 'twixt the heaven and the main,
> Descry a sail.

—a second start as strenuous as the first. The excitement offsets the breaking of the continuity. And the compression of the events, of the storm and the triple landing, then the resolution of the fears for Othello's safety into the happiness of the reuniting of the two—the bringing of all this within the space of a few minutes' acting raises tension to a high pitch and holds it there.

Shakespeare prescriptively makes his storm out of poetry, expands Montano's more or less matter-of-fact

> A fuller blast ne'er shook our battlements:
> If it hath ruffianed so upon the sea,
> What ribs of oak, when mountains melt on them,
> Can hold the mortise?

into the melodious hyperbole of the Second Gentleman's

> For do but stand upon the foaming shore,
> The chiding billow seems to pelt the clouds;
> The wind-shaked surge, with high and monstrous main,
> Seems to cast water on the burning bear,
> And quench the guards of the ever-fixed pole.

descending, however, for Cassio's arrival, and the news he brings, to simpler speech; although the verse with its compelling rhythm —touched, to keep the whole in key, with such an occasional richness of phrase as that which ends Montano's call to the rest to come and scan the sea for a sight of Othello's ship,

> Even till we make the main, and the aerial blue,
> An indistinct regard.

—this is retained. And it lifts again to hyperbole in Cassio's mouth, yet, be it noted, to a quite different tune, for the celebrating of Desdemona's safety:

> Tempests themselves, high seas, and howling winds,
> The guttered rocks, and congregated sands—
> Traitors ensteeped to clog the guiltless keel,
> And having sense of beauty, do omit
> Their mortal natures, letting go safely by
> The divine Desdemona.

and of his hopes for Othello's:

> Great Jove, Othello guard,
> And swell his sail with thine own powerful breath,
> That he may bless this bay with his tall ship. . . .

The scene-painting ends here; for Iago, Desdemona and Emilia appear, and Shakespeare concentrates upon character in action again. Yet these last lines have not been merely decorative. Cassio's fealty to Othello, and his reverence for Desdemona sound in them; points pertinent both to the man and the story. And if treacherous Nature may have spared her for her beauty's sake, we are warned the next instant by the sight of her

> in the conduct of the bold Iago . . .

that man's treachery will not.

The scene's vehemence abates. The storm is forgotten. The verse, deflated of metaphor, flows easily along; and its ease and simplicity benefit Desdemona's own dignity in simplicity and her courageous outward calm. As fittingly, when Iago asserts himself, the verse fractures and disintegrates, after a little, into prose.

But Othello's own safety, still in question, is too important in the story to be left for more postscriptory treatment. So Shakespeare now stimulates suspense by giving no less than a ninety-line stretch of the scene to showing us Desdemona's silent anxiety, which he frames, for emphasis, by contrast, in a bout of artificially comic distraction. The clue to his intention lies in her

> I am not merry; but I do beguile
> The thing I am, by seeming otherwise.

Our attention is centered on her. The chatter and the laughter—hers in forced accord with the rest—and Iago's scurril rhyming are but an incongruous accompaniment to her mutely eloquent fears; and they do not—this we see—by any means beguile her from them. Once the surface of the merriment is pierced by the long-repressed escaping

There's one gone to the harbour?

the sharpness of its anxiety measurable by the comprehending Cassio's kindly reassuring

Ay, madam.

The idle diffuseness of the dialogue, too, by contrast with its recent compression, of itself helps interpret her sense of how time lags while she waits for news.

Iago emerges from the picture (the action must be thought of in terms of Shakespeare's stage[9]) for his malignly vigilant soliloquy:

> He takes her by the palm. Ay, well said, whisper; with as little a web as this, will I ensnare so great a fly as Cassio. . . .

and her share in the scene is reduced to illustrative dumb show; but since she is the subject of the soliloquy she still will hold our attention. The scene's action is here momentarily split, so to speak, into two, its force isolated in the menacingly prominent figure of Iago. Upon his dry explicatory prose the brilliant interruption of the *Trumpet within* tells the more startlingly. Then, with his, Cassio's and Desdemona's combined swift response:

> The Moor! I know his trumpet.
> 'Tis truly so.
> Let's meet him, and receive him.
> Lo, where he comes!

—the whole coheres again, and leaps, unconstrained, to life and movement.

The suspense is over, the tension relaxes. Othello appears; and after the

O, my fair warrior!
My dear Othello!

[9] For his soliloquy he will advance to the front of the main stage; Desdemona and the rest will go towards or into the inner stage, the pictorial effect being of a fully rounded statue placed before a bas-relief.

of their reuniting, comes the nobly fulfilling music of

> It gives me wonder, great as my content,
> To see you here before me. O my soul's joy!
> If after every tempest come such calms,
> May the winds blow till they have wakened death!
> And let the labouring bark climb hills of seas,
> Olympus-high; and duck again as low
> As hell's from heaven! . . .

Here is the scene's third and superlative use of the imagery of the sea. It recalls, too, Desdemona's earlier

> downright violence and storm of fortunes . . .

They have come through both; but only, as we already know—and there is Iago surveying them to remind us of it—into a more treacherous calm. Othello's sequent

> If it were now to die,
> 'Twere now to be most happy; for, I fear,
> My soul hath her content so absolute,
> That not another comfort like to this
> Succeeds in unknown fate.

gives us the already aging, disillusioned man: Desdemona, in her youthfulness, is confident for happiness:

> The heavens forbid
> But that our loves and comforts should increase,
> Even as our days do grow!

And he, inarticulately possessed by love for her, shuts out all but that with a thankful "Amen." For a last minatory jar to the harmony we have the low snarl of Iago's

> O, y'are well tuned now!
> But I'll set down the pegs that make this music,
> As honest as I am.

—and the preparation of the tragedy is complete.[10]

[10] Note that if the editors in general are right—and hardly disputably they are—to follow the lineation of the Quartos, with its

> That e'er our hearts shall make.
> O you are well tuned now. . . .

then the scansion dictates this dovetailed and much elided "O, y'are . . ." and the unescapable snarl in it.

IAGO COMPASSES CASSIO'S DOWNFALL

Iago sets to work without delay; and for long to come now he will seldom be absent from the scene, since, fittingly, the action is centered on him, woven round him, even as he himself, spider-like, weaves its plot. But the attempt upon Othello will be no trifling matter, and Shakespeare lets us see him proving his quality first upon lesser and less dangerous game. His vague plan "engendered" in Venice—

> After some time, to abuse Othello's ear . . .

with scandal about Cassio and Desdemona—is consequently now shaped for a start to a prompter disgrace of Cassio, to an immediate profit by that;

> To get his place . . .

—so much to go on with!

We have sampled his protean gifts already with the transforming of the raucous cloaked figure beneath Brabantio's balcony into the frank, conscientious soldier, this again into Roderigo's coolly sceptic mentor in vice. From which nearest seeming semblance of himself it is that he now starts again, to turn, even more easily, jolly companion with Cassio, then moralist with Montano, before Othello to be once more the loyal soldier, and so on and so forth—swift to respond to the occasion's demand on him. He buys his way ahead with unstinted false coin. But the display is divided by soliloquies in which his naked mind can be seen and the course he is steering shown us, and, since he steers from point to point only, by no less than four.

Roderigo is to be his instrument; and upon the instructions which emerge from the web of words he habitually weaves about this feeblest of his victims—

> Watch you to-night; for the command, I'll lay't upon you. . . . do you find some occasion to anger Cassio, either by speaking too loud, or tainting his discipline; or from what other course you please. . . . Sir, he is rash and very sudden in choler; and, haply, with his truncheon may strike at you. Provoke him, that he may. . . .

—upon this precise priming of our expectation Shakespeare can afford the halt in the action of the Herald's proclamation.

The proclamation in itself serves several subsidiary purposes. It helps settle the characters in Cyprus. The chances and excitements of the arrival are over. Othello is in command; but the war is over too, and he only needs bid the people rejoice at peace and his happy marriage. It economically sketches us a background for Cassio's ill-fated carouse. It allows a small breathing-space before Iago definitely gets to work. It "neutralizes" the action for a moment (a Herald is an anonymous voice; he has no individuality), suspends its interest without breaking its continuity. Also it brings its present timelessness to an end; events are given a clock to move by, and with that take on a certain urgency.[11]

Now comes

Enter Othello, Desdemona, Cassio, and Attendants.

The *Attendants*, which is the Folio's addition, add a touch of ceremony to this brief passage across the stage. But while it is no more, the few lines it allows for, with their easy cadence—

> Good Michael, look you to the guard to-night.
> Let's teach ourselves that honourable stop,
> Not to outsport discretion.

—are economically made to speak of the effortless discipline which shows the good soldier in Othello, of his own temperance and self-discipline, of his affection too, as they flow on, for Cassio; "Michael" twice over. Shakespeare sounds the quiet note of the normal while he may; the strenuous action to come will tell the better against it.

Upon Othello's verse and the melodious echo of its final rhymed couplet impinges Iago's brisk prose, and his gross talk of

[11] But a clock whose hands move to order, so to speak. The Herald refers to "this present hour of five." A dozen lines later Iago says, " 'Tis not yet ten o' th' clock." Modern editors isolate the Herald's speech as a separate scene; and the cleared stage before and after it justifies this, and overcomes—over-overcomes, one may say—the incongruity of the leap in time. The Quartos, as usual, make no such indications. The stage is twice cleared, in fact; the effect is made. What need in print to call attention to the matter? It is only worth remarking that the editor of the Folio, inserting scene-divisions, establishes one before the speech, where no incongruity of time is in question, but not after, when, if the point could have troubled him, it is.

Desdemona strikes a yet more flagrant contrast to the uncalculated dignity of the little wedding procession we have seen pass by. Cassio in his devout admiration of her—the more incredible, by these repeated signs of it, any notion of their adultery!—is coldly unresponsive, would positively protest (we may feel, and the actor can indicate) but for his manly reluctance—upon which Iago impishly plays—to be branded Puritan. It is a like shamefacedness, a dearly-to-be-requited dash of petty moral cowardice, which betrays him a moment later in the matter of the "brace of Cyprus gallants" and "the stoup of wine."

The technical utility of Iago's sixteen-line soliloquy, which fills the gap between Cassio's departure to "call them in" and his return with them and Montano, is to allow time for the "rouse" which will bring him back a step or so advanced in tipsiness already. For, since we are to have his repentance set out at length, we do not need to see the full process of his undoing besides. Shakespeare may seem to be short of pertinent material here. We are told that the feeble Roderigo has been fortified for his provocative task with a little Dutch courage too; this apart, no more than within a minute, we shall see for ourselves. But the soliloquy brings us at this ripe instant into naked touch again with Iago's quick, confident mind. And, cast for speed and impetus (by contrast with the surrounding prose) in easily flowing verse, with its final couplet—

> If consequence do but approve my dream,
> My boat sails freely, both with wind and stream.

—it whips up the scene to the spirited pitch at which Cassio's exuberantly hilarious

> Fore God, they have given me a rouse already.

is to capture it.

A tavern would, of course, be the suitable place for the carouse which follows, and the action could quite easily be transported there. But Shakespeare prefers to concentrate it all in this convenient nowhere in particular, so that it may come and go around Iago, its General in Command—who need not, therefore, now, nor for the rest of the long scene, quit the stage, nor have to relax his hold on it or us, until this battle is won and his next planned. The essentials of a tavern are as easily transported here; and a joke about the English being "most potent in potting" and a couple of ditties "learned in England" will—with an English audience—assure the illusion.

There is an edge to the foolery. As Cassio grows ridiculous in his cups Iago covertly mocks him, fanning his own jealous enmity too, with repetition of the respectful "lieutenant," "good lieutenant" (for how little longer will he need to call him so!), luring him to the jocular patronage of

> the lieutenant is to be saved before the ancient. . . . this is my ancient. . . .

—more food for enmity there! This flares out with Montano for one incautious moment in the contemptuous

> You see this fellow, that is gone before. . . .

flung after his "good lieutenant's" unsteady departure to set the watch, to be as quickly masked again, however, beneath kindly, comradely—but how poisonously seasoned!—reprobation:

> He is a soldier fit to stand by Cæsar
> And give direction; and do but see his vice. . . .

Another drop here into somewhat laden verse lends the passage sententious gravity; and the artless Montano is prompt to respond. For a signal of what is now imminent, Roderigo, drifting tipsily into the scene, is shot off upon his errand, is here and is gone—so swift can Iago be at a crisis—while Montano takes breath between sentences. And in another minute the mine has been sprung, and riot is afoot, with Montano also, by brilliant afterthought, involved.

Amid clamor and clangor, shouts, swords and the "dreadful bell" outtopping all, Othello appears, attended as before—by *Gentlemen with weapons*, say the Quartos; this helps depict him ruler of Cyprus. It is the second time that, by a word or so, he, the soldier, stops, not forwards, a fight. Calm restored, he begins his sternly quiet questioning: first of Iago, who looks "dead with grieving," and so is plainly a witness, not a partaker, yet answers the "Who began this?" with a frank "I do not know"—leaving the culprits scope to damnify themselves the more; next of Cassio, too shamed to speak; then of Montano, disabled by his wound. Then it is Iago's turn again, and he has only—how conveniently!—to speak the truth. He gives it convincing clarity and circumstance, falsifies it ever so slightly. It is not the whole truth, that is all. Othello's sentence follows:

> I know, Iago,
> Thy honesty and love doth mince this matter,
> Making it light to Cassio—Cassio, I love thee;
> But never more be officer of mine.

Its place in the story besides, the episode serves the unfolding of his character. Here is the heroic calm still, but with a dangerous stirring beneath:

> Now, by heaven,
> My blood begins my safer guides to rule;
> And passion, having my best judgment collied,
> Assays to lead the way. . . .

Iago and the broken Cassio are left alone. There is a moment's silence (marked after the tumult and the coming and going of guards and onlookers) while Iago quizzically surveys his handiwork. No stage direction is needed to indicate this. It is written into the text, with its breaking by the feline

> What, are you hurt, lieutenant?

—he still, most considerately, calls him "lieutenant."

There is nothing of the tragic hero in Cassio. He is as human in his repentance as in his folly, somewhat ridiculous—most enjoyably so to Iago—in the facility of his despair and the amplitude of his self-reproach, in such hyperbole as

> O thou invisible spirit of wine, if thou hast no name to be known by, let us call thee devil.

Iago, making sure by one shrewd question that his own tracks are covered, lets all this wear itself out; then, "in the sincerity of love and honest kindness," gives him the fatal advice, gratefully accepted, to importune Desdemona to plead for him with Othello, and, not omitting another cryptically ironic "lieutenant" or two, sends him away somewhat comforted. He has steered back to the main lines of his plan:

> After some time, to abuse Othello's ear . . .

with means now provided.

The soliloquy which follows:

> And what's he then that says I play the villain? . . .

is a nodal point in the play, and it adds an essential to the viability of Iago's character. Until now he has been self-seeking; and Cassio's lieutenancy is surely in sight. But how will Desdemona's ruin profit him? It is evil for its own sake that he starts pursuing now; and out of her very goodness he will

> make the net
> That shall enmesh them all.

—with which enrichment of wickedness opens a darker depth of tragedy by far.[12]

Here too would plainly be a striking finish to this long scene. But Shakespeare provides Iago instead with another exhilarating bout with Roderigo, who returns sobered—he also—by his beating, crestfallen and peevish. A few platitudes appease him. Iago has no further use for him; he has served his turn. But the despised little nincompoop will trip up his betrayer yet. That is the significance of his reappearance. He is dispatched to billet and bed. Iago, we note, needs no rest. The sun is rising. He also departs, briskly confident of adding to a good night's work a better day's.

THE ATTACK UPON OTHELLO

For relaxation before the tense main business of the tragedy begins we next have Cassio in the early morning bringing musicians to play beneath Othello's window (a pleasant custom, and here what delicate amends!), to this being added the grosser, conventional japes of the Clown. The few minutes so spent are offset by the unexpectedly close knitting of the main action when this begins again. For Iago finds no need to "set on" his wife to

> move for Cassio to her mistress . . .

Cassio having saved him thus much trouble by making bold (he is sadly humbled, so to appeal to the waiting-gentlewoman) to send in to her himself. And she comes to report that Desdemona,

[12] This soliloquy is more fully discussed in the section on the play's characters, p. 105.

unasked, is already speaking for him "stoutly." The economical compression strengthens the tension of the scene, and the fortuitous furthering of Iago's ends bodingly suggests to us besides that the luck is with him.

For two last strokes of preparation we have Cassio, with the weak man's impatience, bent on importuning Desdemona to do for him what he has been told she is doing already, begging Emilia to gain him the

advantage of some brief discourse . . .

with her alone, and a passing sight of Othello, at his general's task, Iago beside him, effectively promoted lieutenant already.

Then we see Cassio with Desdemona; but not alone. Emilia is there, it is before Emilia that she promises to help him. Upon them, after a—for us—expectant minute or so comes Othello. Iago has not, needless to say, drawn him "out of the way" as he told Cassio he would, but back here to find the two; Emilia's unexpected presence, he can show, a slight vexation to him. And it is in the midst of these indeterminate comings and goings that his muttered

Ha! I like not that.

so effectively sows the seed—this tiniest of seeds—of tragedy.

The Ambiguity in Time: A Parenthesis

It is from this point, too, that the action passes into the ambiguity of time which has troubled so many critics. Compression of time, by one means or another, is common form in drama, and we have just seen it put to use in the speeding through a single unbroken scene of the whole night of Cassio's betrayal. But now comes—if we are examining the craft of the play—something more complex. When it is acted we notice nothing unusual, and neither story nor characters appear false in retrospect. It is as with the perspective of a picture, painted to be seen from a certain standpoint. Picture and play can be enjoyed and much of their art appreciated with no knowledge of how the effect is gained. But the student needs to know.

We have reached the morrow of the arrival in Cyprus and of

the consummation of the marriage. This is plain. It is morning. By the coming midnight or a little later Othello will have murdered Desdemona and killed himself. To that measure of time, as plainly demonstrated, the rest of the play's action will move. It comprises no more than seven scenes. From this early hour we pass without interval—the clock no more than customarily speeded—to midday dinner-time and past it.[13] Then comes a break in the action (an empty stage; one scene ended, another beginning), which, however, can only allow for a quite inconsiderable interval of time, to judge, early in the following scene, by Desdemona's "Where should I lose that handkerchief, Emilia?" —the handkerchief which we have recently seen Emilia retrieve and pass to Iago. And later in this scene Cassio gives it to Bianca, who begs that she may see him "soon at night." Then comes another break in the action. But, again, it can involve no long interval of time; since in the scene following Bianca speaks of the handkerchief given her "even now." Later in the scene Lodovico, suddenly come from Venice, is asked by Othello to supper; and between Cassio and Bianca there has been more talk of "tonight" and "supper." Another break in the action; but, again, little or no passing of time can be involved, since midway through the next scene the trumpets sound to supper, and Iago closes it with

> It is now high supper-time and the night grows to waste. . . .

The following scene opens with Othello, Desdemona and Lodovico coming from supper, with Othello's command to Desdemona:

> Get you to bed on the instant. . . .

and ends with her good-night to Emilia. The scene after—of the ambush for Cassio—we have been explicitly told is to be made by Iago to "fall out between twelve and one," and it is, we find, pitch dark, and the town is silent. And from here Othello and Emilia patently go straight to play their parts in the last scene of all, he first, she later, as quickly as she can speed.[14]

---

[13] Midday is not specified, but it was the usual dinner hour.

[14] The suggestion is, moreover, that in point of time, these two last scenes overlap; and, since the scene of Cassio's ambush moves so swiftly and that of Desde-

These, then, are the events of a single day; and Shakespeare is at unusual pains to make this clear, by the devices of the morning music, dinner-time, supper-time and the midnight dark, and their linking together by the action itself and reference after reference in the dialogue. Nor need we have any doubt of his reasons for this. Only by thus precipitating the action can it be made both effective in the terms of his stagecraft and convincing. If Othello were left time for reflection or the questioning of anyone but Iago, would not the whole flimsy fraud that is practiced on him collapse?

But this granted, are they convincing as the events of that particular day, the very morrow of the reunion and of the consummation of the marriage?[15] Plainly they will not be; and before long Shakespeare has begun to imply that we are weeks or months—or it might be a year or more—away from anything of the sort.

> What sense had I of her stolen hours of lust?
> I saw it not, thought it not; it harmed not me;
> I slept the next night well, was free and merry;
> I found not Cassio's kisses on her lips. . . .

mona's murder, to begin with, so slowly, this suggestion can be brought home to the audience. Quite early in the first of the two we have Othello's

> Strumpet, I come! . . .

And, during the scuffling and confusion, the stabbing of Roderigo, Bianca's bewailings, Emilia's scoldings, he is already—and the precipitancy of his departure will have implied it—with Desdemona and about his deadly work. By the scene's end, therefore, and Iago's

> Emilia, run you to the citadel. . . .

(which we shall not have forgotten when we hear her next knocking at the bedroom door) it is too late.

[15] Determination to find a possible gap in the action by which Iago's attack on Othello is entirely postponed by some weeks or months can only be rewarded by doing violence to the slight break in continuity between Emilia's offer to conduct Cassio to Desdemona with a "Pray you, come in," and Desdemona's reception of him with the

> Be then assured, good Cassio, I will do
> All my abilities in thy behalf.

And nothing can be plainer, by Elizabethan stagecraft, than a (thus much interrupted) passage here from outer stage to inner, with Othello's passage across the outer stage—

> These letters give, Iago, to the pilot. . . .
> This fortification, gentlemen, shall we see't?

—for a connecting link.

That is evidence enough, but a variety of other implications go to confirm it; Iago's

> I lay with Cassio lately. . . .

Cassio's reference to his "former suit," Bianca's reproach to him

> What, keep a week away? seven days and nights?
> Eight score eight hours? . . .

More pointedly yet, Lodovico's arrival from Venice with the mandate of recall, the war being over—by every assumption of the sort, indeed, Othello and Desdemona and the rest are living the life of Cinthio's episodic story, not at the forced pace of Shakespeare's play. But he wants to make the best of both these calendars; and, in his confident, reckless, dexterous way, he contrives to do so.

Why, however, does he neglect the obvious and simple course of allowing a likely lapse of time between the night of Cassio's disgrace and the priming of Othello to suspect Desdemona and her kindness to him—for which common sense, both our own, and, we might suppose, Iago's, cries out? The answer is that there has been one such break in the action already, forced on him by the voyage to Cyprus, and he must avoid another.

The bare Elizabethan stage bred a panoramic form of drama; the story straightforwardly unfolded, as many as possible of its incidents presented, narrative supplying the antecedents and filling the gaps. Its only resources of any value are the action itself and the speech, and the whole burden, therefore, of stimulating and sustaining illusion falls on the actor—who, once he has captured his audience, must, like the spell-binding orator he may in method much resemble, be at pains to hold them, or a part of his work will be frequently to do again. Our mere acceptance of the fiction, of the story and its peopling—we shall perhaps not withdraw; we came prepared to accept it. Something subtler is involved; the sympathy (in the word's stricter sense) which the art of the actor will have stirred in us. This current interrupted by the suspension of the action is not to be automatically restored by its resumption. Our emotions, roused and let grow cold, must be roused again—and swiftly too, if, as in this play, emotion is to be a screen for liberties taken with the logic of the story's conduct. And the effects of such forced stoking will stale with repetition, until, if the actor in difficulties be tempted to coarsen the process too much, in its crudity it may fail of effect altogether.

Hence the help to the Elizabethan actor, with so much dependent on him, of continuity of action. Having captured his audience, he can the better hope to hold it. The dramatist may profit too. He will be spared the bridging of gaps by accounts of events intervening; secondary or superfluous matter, low in tension. Shakespeare hereabouts evades this aspect of the voyage to Cyprus and its inconveniences by ignoring them, and by restarting the divided action amid the stimulating—and effacing—anxieties of the storm. But such another—and necessarily a not too similar—device would be hard to find. Were he, moreover, to allow that likely lapse of time before the attack on Othello's confidence is even begun, it would but suggest to us as we watch the equal likelihood of an aptly scheming Iago letting at least a day or two pass between each assault to give his poison time to work. And with that the whole dramatic fabric would begin to crumble. Here would be Cinthio's circumspect Ensign again, and he would leave the action stagnating, with more gaps to be bridged, more intervening events to be accounted for, if ever so cursorily, the onrush of Othello's passion checked and checked again, and he given time to reflect and anyone the opportunity to enlighten him! Give Othello such respite; and if he then does not, by the single stroke of good sense needed, free himself from the fragile web of lies which is choking him, he will seem to be simply the gull and dolt "as ignorant as dirt" of Emilia's final invective, no tragic hero, certainly.

Shakespeare has to work within the close confines of the dramatic form; and this imposes on him a strict economy in the shaping of means to end and end to means, of characters to the action and the action to the characters. If Othello's ruin is not accomplished without pause or delay, it can hardly, under the circumstances, be accomplished at all. This predicates an Iago of swift and reckless decision (qualities that, again, the compression of time both demands and heightens) that will both win him his barren triumph and ensure his downfall. Then, again, Othello's precipitate fall from height to depth is tragically appropriate to the man he is—as to the man he is made because the fall must be precipitate. And that we may rather feel with Othello in his suffering than despise him for the folly of it, *we* are speeded through time as unwittingly as he is, and left little more chance for reflection.

Not, however, that continuity of action is of use simply for the sustaining of tension, nor that, continuity being kept, tension must not on occasion be relaxed; for if it were not—and fairly often—the strain, in any play highly charged with emotion, would become intolerable. But the dramatist can better regulate this necessary ebb and flow and turn it to account in the course of the action itself than if it is obstructed by repeated stopping and starting.

In all this, truly, Shakespeare treats time itself most unconscionably. But he smooths incongruities away by letting the action follow the hourly calendar without more comment than is necessary, while he takes the longer one for granted in incidental references. And all is well while he sees that the two do not clash in any positive contradiction.

The change into ambiguity of time is effected in the course of Iago's first and decisive attack upon Othello. This is divided into two, with the summons to dinner and the finding and surrender of the handkerchief for an interlude. In the earlier part—although it is taken for granted—there is no very definite reference to the longer calendar, and Iago, until towards the end of it, deals only in generalities.[16] Not until the second part do we have the determinate "I lay with Cassio lately. . . ," the story of his dream, the matter of the handkerchief, and Othello's own

> I slept the next night well, was free and merry;
> I found not Cassio's kisses on her lips. . . .

with its implication of passing weeks or months after the morrow of the landing. But would it not also in reason be the better for the suggestion of some longer interval, during which Iago's doses of poison will have had more chance to work, than the dinner

---

[16] There is, however, one earlier incidental sign that the longer calendar is already in Shakespeare's mind, Desdemona's reference to Cassio as

> A man that languishes in your displeasure . . .

—"languishes" certainly suggesting something more than a few hours of disgrace.

to "the generous islanders" can offer? But here arises again the question of continuity of action. A suggested interval would not only, from the standpoint of reason, seem to give the poison time to work but some antidote of good sense too. And from the standpoint of the play's action, such an interruption, actual or suggested, must lower its tension and dissipate interest, just when its main business, moreover, too long held back, is fairly under way. Shakespeare will certainly not feel called on to make such a sacrifice to the reasonabilities. Lowering it but a very little, he does break the tension upon Othello's and Desdemona's departure (Emilia left behind, the scene continuing, the continuity of action kept). He inserts the episode of the handkerchief. Treated by Iago, this will capture our interest. Then Othello returns, transformed from the man merely troubled in mind to a creature incapable of reason, "eaten up with passion . . ."; and a little of his emotion reflected in us will let us too lose count of time, obliterate yesterday in today, confound the weeks with the months in the one intolerable moment.

But the overriding explanation of what Shakespeare does here and at similar junctures is that he is not essentially concerned with time and the calendar at all. These, as with the actor and his behavior, and other outward circumstances, must be given plausibility. But the play's essential action lies in the processes of thought and feeling by which the characters are moved and the story is forwarded. And the deeper the springs of these the less do time, place and circumstance affect them. His imagination is now concerned with fundamental passions, and its swift working demands uncumbered expression. He may falsify the calendar for his convenience, but we shall find neither trickery nor anomaly in the fighting of the intellectual battle for Othello's soul. And in the light of the truth of this the rest will pass unnoticed.

Examination of the Play's Shaping, Resumed

At no other moment than this, when she is pleading for Cassio with Othello, do we see Desdemona quite confidently, carelessly happy. She could beguile her fears for Othello's safe landing by laughing with the rest at Iago's sallies; but it was empty laughter. Into the ecstasy of their reuniting had stolen his boding

> If it were now to die,
> 'Twere now to be most happy. . . .

Their first wedded intimacy was marred by the alarms of the broil. And when a little later she comes to call him in to dinner, the rift between them—though she does not know it—will have opened. Even with the tale of his headache and her

> I'm very sorry that you are not well.

her gaiety has gone.

Shakespeare gives himself this single chance, then, of showing her, and Othello too, as they well might have hoped so happily to be. The picture is drawn in a few strokes; in her youthfully generous impatience of the discipline which makes Cassio "an example"; in the hinted sense of his—for her—elderliness in the

> 'Tis as I should entreat you wear your gloves,
> Or feed on nourishing dishes, or keep you warm. . . .

in his uxorious yielding and her sensitive response to the gently measured irony which covers it:

> I will deny thee nothing:
> Whereon, I do beseech thee, grant me this,
> To leave me but a little to myself.

with the tender

> Be as your fancies teach you;
> Whate'er you be, I am obedient.

—its pretty singsong only sharpening for us its unconsciously tragic presage. Her artless pride, too, in her new power of place as her "great captain's captain," shows in the bidding Cassio stay to hear her speak, with its confidence that then and there she can "bring him in." And her importunity seems so to publish her innocence that, as Iago stands watching the two of them—his first move, the muttered mock-impulsive "Ha! I like not that," already made—we may well ask ourselves whatever matter for a second he will manage to find.[17] Desdemona provides it him. For it is from her mischievously merry

What! Michael Cassio,
That came a-wooing with you, and so many a time,
When I have spoke of you dispraisingly . . .

that he draws his

My noble lord . . .
Did Michael Cassio, when you woo'd my lady,
Know of your love?[18]

Iago, it will be remembered, is now playing for deadlier stakes than Cassio's lieutenancy. His net is to "enmesh them all"; and while so far he has had no more precise end in view, the evil possessing him is no longer of the sort to be appeased by material gain. Nor has he, in fact, the means of inflicting such disaster on Othello. To whom could he betray him as he has betrayed Cassio? He must bring him to be the cause of his own undoing.

Before he provokes his passions Iago means to corrupt his mind. How to set about this? Not by direct assault; he cannot deal with him as with a Roderigo. Here too there must be self-destruction. The best he can do to begin with is to find some flaw in the moral defense, some little leak in the dike, and quietly contrive to enlarge it. Othello has unquestioning self-confidence. Yet he is no egoist; he translates this spontaneously into confidence

[17] The stagecraft hereabouts is presumably as follows: Desdemona, Emilia and Cassio are on the inner stage, where Cassio has been brought ("in") by Emilia for the beginning of the scene, for which the curtains will probably have been drawn back also. Othello and Iago enter on the outer stage. They re-enter rather; and the Quartos have them still accompanied by the gentlemen who went with them, a while since, to the fortifications, and who will now, after a moment or so, vanish unnoticed. That the Quartos should not allow them an exeunt is nothing out of the way, and the only slight importance in their return is that it strengthens the continuity of the action. The outer stage now serves the purpose of a sort of anteroom (the modern editorial *Enter Othello and Iago at a distance* has no specific warrant; we owe it to Theobald apparently), and this will account for Othello catching only a glimpse of Cassio as he leaves. It looks as if Othello was then meant to join Desdemona, momentarily at least, upon the inner stage while Iago remains in the "anteroom," removed from them at any rate, and free, while he watches them, to give expressive play to his thoughts.

[18] Additional evidence of his eavesdropping from the "anteroom." Had he been an open listener to their talk he would be asking a question of which he obviously already knew the answer.

in others. But the more unquestioningly it has been given the harder will any breach made in it be to restore; and to loss of confidence in the culprit will be added some latent loss of self-confidence too. He loved Cassio and his confidence in him was betrayed. He may forgive him; but not only can he never feel sure of him again, by just so much he will remain the less sure of himself. Here is a leak in the dike, which Desdemona by her pleading has already done something to enlarge; for Othello is yielding to her against his better judgment.

One way, and a swift one, to the corrupting of the mind is through a perverting of the imagination. Othello's is, even as his nature is, full-powered. But he has exercised it in spiritual solitude, and for that it is the less sophisticated and the more easily to be victimized by alien suggestion. Again, he must be induced to do himself the harm; and Iago, as the process is here illustrated and compressed, begins with words as bait; and, so to speak, he trails these words before him, sapping their integrity by questionable stress and intonation, by iteration lending them a cumulative power, setting imagination to confuse and falsify the plain thoughts which they should represent. It is a poetic practice bedeviled, and he is expert in it. And in the ensuing doubt and confusion he can the better operate.[19]

Forthwith, in answer to the sequent question he prompts Othello to ask him, he strikes the keynote of—

> But for a satisfaction of my thought . . .

augmenting it with the pejorative

> No further harm.

The combination vibrates in Othello's ear; and a rapidly reciprocated "thought . . . thought . . . think," with an echo of Desdemona's "honest" from her

> I have no judgment in an honest face. . . .

for reinforcement, issues in

> What dost thou think?
>
> Think, my lord?
>
> Think, my lord!

[19] The student may find it convenient to have these passages of close analysis accompanied by the pertinent part of the text itself.

By heaven, he echoes me,
As if there were some monster in his thought
Too hideous to be shown.

—imagination both intrigued and balked. Iago's tacit pose provokes it further, and to the appeal:

if thou dost love me,
Show me thy thought.
My lord, you know I love you.

The feint at evasion can but halt before Othello's own unequivocal

I think thou dost. . . .

and in a moment the opportunity is offered of

For Michael Cassio,
I dare be sworn—I think that he is honest.

its shift from "sworn" to "think," doubling the dubiety of "think," making it the most provocative stroke yet.

The disintegrating play of word and thought continues. Iago, like a tricky wrestler, slips and dodges, evades and invites attack, nor lets himself be cornered until, upon the imperative

I'll know thy thoughts.

he retorts with the defiant

You cannot, if my heart were in your hand;
Nor shall not, whilst 'tis in my custody.

and coolly casts loose, sure that he at least has stirred Othello's imagination into a turmoil, riddled his mind with doubts.

He is skirmishing ahead behind this screen of word-play. Emerging, who still could be more disinterested, scrupulous, more benevolent than Iago? Trust in Cassio is inevitably flawed, with none but himself to blame. But no slur has yet been cast on Desdemona; unless an intonation in the sententious

Good name in man *and woman*, dear my lord,
Is the immediate jewel of their souls. . . .

should strike Othello's sharpening ear. And the envenoming "jealousy" is first insinuated, incidentally, as self-reproach:

it is my nature's plague
To spy into abuses, and oft my jealousy
Shapes faults that are not. . . .

Confessing to our faults wins confidence. How, after that, should simplicity of heart suspect in a fervent warning—

O, beware, my lord, of jealousy. . . .

—the poisonous suggestion from which jealousy may breed?

Iago quickly slips back into the impersonal upon his homilectic "green-eyed monster. . . ." But the sting of the brutal "cuckold"—of the word itself and the very sound of it—will rankle, and to the invitation of the final "jealousy" Othello responds.

It is an encouragingly defenseless response; in the murmured "O, misery!", which Iago may rather surmise than hear, yet more so in the superficial confidence, the disdain, the apparently robust good sense of

Why, why is this?
Think'st thou I'ld make a life of jealousy. . . ?

—as you, Iago, confess you do.

'Tis not to make me jealous,
To say my wife is fair, feeds well, loves company,
Is free of speech, sings, plays, and dances well. . . .
I'll see before I doubt; when I doubt, prove;
And, on the proof, there is no more but this,
Away at once with love or jealousy!

But it is all too positive; the protestations are too elaborate; that "jealousy" sticks in his mind like a burr, and will to the tip of his tongue. And for the first time "my wife" is specifically brought into the question. Nor does he take in the least amiss his friend Iago's interference in the matter. He ends, indeed, with a tacit invitation, something foolhardily like a challenge to him, to go further if he can. It is a challenge which Iago readily accepts.

Hereabouts, in terms of actual life, he might more wisely be breaking off this first successful engagement, to return later to the attack with his gains consolidated, when the intellectual poison shall have spread, and the self-infecting fever of the imagination risen higher yet. Shakespeare, for reasons we have argued, does not commonly permit himself such gaps; but their admissible places are often traceable in the close-knit fabric by little—for a simile—knots and splicings where the threads change color or thickness.

So here. Iago, thus encouraged (as he says) by his equanimity, by (as we see) Othello's ill-concealed trepidation, shows his "love and duty" to his "dear . . . lord" with a "franker spirit" indeed. Desdemona is no longer "my lady"; we have the bluntly familiar

Look to your wife. . . .

instead, which quickly leads, by way of the insidious

I know our country disposition well. . . .

(hint at the alien in Othello and the seed of much misgiving) to the first thrust home:

> She did deceive her father, marrying you;
> And when she seemed to shake and fear your looks,
> She loved them most.

A twofold accusation; both aspects of it actually true; her very love for Othello turned seamy side without. A most apt thrust. And back to his mind must come—to ours also, for the moment was memorable—Brabantio's

> Look to her, Moor, have a quick eye to see;
> She has deceived her father, and may thee.

The very words; Iago had heard them.

The tormentor, from now on, has his prey intellectually broken in, and answering, compliantly or by recoil, to each touch on the rein, each flick of the whip; to such a show of unctuous devotion as the hardy mind would repel by a pitiable

I am bound to thee for ever.

to the covertly derisive

I see this hath a little dashed your spirits.

by the hollow

Not a jot, not a jot.

And he winces now at the very name of Cassio.

He must be brought to admitting his distress, to fettering it on himself, so to say. Iago reiterates, therefore, the

My lord, I see you're moved.

and is repaid by the converting of that earlier, elaborate, dignified disclaimer into the feeble protest that he is

> not much moved . . .

while a return to the perplexity of

> I do not think but Desdemona's honest.

(but it is Desdemona now, not Cassio!) shows that incipient poison to be still at work. How should Iago then resist the veiled sarcasm of

> Long live she so! And long live you to think so!

The next opening Othello volunteers:

> And yet, how nature erring from itself—

It seems to betoken a disquiet dilating more profoundly in him. Iago boldly takes advantage of it. Too boldly? he asks himself—when he has tarred Desdemona with

> a will most rank,
> Foul disproportion, thoughts unnatural . . .

—and he sidles into qualifying apologies, managing to make them, however, yet more damagingly to the point.

> though I may fear
> Her will, recoiling to her better judgment,
> May fail to match you with her country forms,
> And happily repent.[20]

But he need have felt no misgiving. Othello's

> Farewell, farewell . . .

is friendly, although he will not be deceived by its ostensible carelessness, nor by the offhand

> If more thou dost perceive, let me know more. . . .

[20] "Will," in one of its senses, connotes carnal appetite. For us it has lost that meaning, so we lose here the effect of its use. Of what Iago means and would be understood to mean there is no doubt. But if Othello were to turn upon him he could plead the ambiguity of the word (Shakespeare continually plays upon it: for the most cited instance, see Sonnets 134-6) and take refuge in one of its politer senses. "Happily" the O.E.D. allows may stand for "haply."

Nor indeed can Othello sustain this. Despite himself there breaks from him the shameful

Set on thy wife to observe. . . .

—hard upon its heels the curt

leave me, Iago.

confessing the shame. And Iago himself must find it difficult to keep some coloring of exultation out of the obedient

My lord, I take my leave.

Is he wise to return as he does instead of letting well alone? It is as if he could not keep his fingers off this instrument which now yields so fascinatingly to his touch. But he wants to make sure that in his absence the good work will go on, Cassio be held off, so that Desdemona in her innocence *may* "strain his entertainment," while Othello, primed just to this degree of suspicion, will watch them but say nothing—since, of course, a few frank words to either could still cut through the flimsy net. He meets, for response, with a stiff

Fear not my government.

But he is not deceived by the studied dignity of that.

Othello, the man of action, is not habitually introspective, and Shakespeare allots him this single true soliloquy. He is used neither to concealing nor analyzing his own thoughts and motives, nor to conjecturing other men's. He is quite childishly impressed by Iago's cleverness at that—who

doubtless
Sees and knows more, much more, than he unfolds.

who

knows all qualities, with a learned spirit,
Of human dealings.

But he, his faith attacked, his imagination poisoned, his mind perplexed, and now alone, is a man spiritually rudderless and adrift. He surrenders first to panic:

If I do prove her haggard,
Though that her jesses were my dear heart-strings,
I'ld whistle her off, and let her down the wind
To prey at fortune.

next, pathetically, to the humbling thought:

> Haply, for I am black
> And have not those soft parts of conversation
> That chamberers have, or that I am declined
> Into the vale of years—yet that's not much . . .

then to precipitate despair:

> She's gone; I am abused, and my relief
> Must be to loathe her.

—relief finding its immediate expression in such commonplace sarcasms as the idealist turned misogynist will habitually have at call, talk of "this forked plague" and the like.

Then the mere sight of Desdemona—no more than that needed to dissipate these figments!—seems to be about to make all well. Yet to her simple, happily intimate

> How now, my dear Othello!
> Your dinner, and the generous islanders
> By you invited, do attend your presence.

he finds himself—despite himself—responding only with sardonically riddling evasions. The wedge of suspicion has been driven between them.

The soliloquy and this brief passage between the two form a trough in the waves of the action, allowing us a survey of Othello as Iago's first attack has left him; passions not yet fired, but mind and imagination bewildered and warped, confidence gone.

THE HANDKERCHIEF

The two depart to their "duty" dinner with "the generous islanders," and then follows the quick exchange between Iago and Emilia over the handkerchief. Thick-skinned Emilia's unscannable

> I am glad I have found this napkin. . . .

is matched, as for contrast, against the gentle melody of Desdemona's parting line. Iago comes prowling, alert for Othello's return, to vent petty spleen on his wife because he finds her here instead (that much of safety valve he may allow himself);

offering amends with a brutally indecent joke, quibbled away. Her indifference to such usage, her concern to gratify him! Her discrimination in dishonesty:

> What handkerchief?
> Why, that the Moor first gave to Desdemona,
> That which so often you did bid me steal.
> Hast stolen it from her?
> No, faith; she let it drop by negligence,
> And, to the advantage, I being here took't up. . . .

and her shruggingly submissive departure at his curt bidding! Here is a pair united by very different bonds.

This makes but a forty-line interlude between Othello's departure, deeply disquieted, it is true, yet self-controlled still, and his return, a creature possessed. Nor does Shakespeare mitigate the inordinacy of the contrast by any pretended spinning-out of time or incidental change of subject, or shift of place. He does not even shift from verse to prose, and tension is fully sustained. But there is both surprise and substance in this episode of the handkerchief, and enough of both to secure our complete attention. So it serves equally as a solid division between the two capital scenes and as a firm bridge uniting them.

Its pettiness, besides, will throw into relief the toweringly tragic force of what is to come. Iago stresses this for us with his

> Trifles light as air
> Are to the jealous confirmations strong
> As proofs of holy writ: this may do something. . . .

That it can be made to do what it does, a handkerchief found by chance and filched, that in such a trifle such deadly power can be lodged—men's lives at its mercy!—is, of course, the dramatic point of its use. The poignancy of the tragedy gains by contrast with the pettiness. Further, a spice of sheer ill-luck is involved, and this relieves the severity of what has now become a tragedy of character, with its ordered cause and effect steadily pointing and leading to the justified end.[21]

[21] It is instinctive to compare the part played in the story by this episode with the piece of unalloyed ill-luck by which, in *Romeo and Juliet*, Friar John's journey to Mantua is stayed. By that and that only the play's catastrophe is precipitated. Shakespeare has much matured in art since then. In Cinthio's story the Ensign

Iago continues:

> The Moor already changes with my poison:
> Dangerous conceits are in their natures poisons,
> Which at the first are scarce found to distaste,
> But with a little act upon the blood
> Burn like the mines of sulphur.

This is the effective link between his late encounter with Othello and the one to come, and it shows signs of being arbitrarily compressed to make it so. "The Moor already changes. . . ."—a hint here that Iago has come from watching him, just possible to suggest in action, amid this telescoping of time (if he came from the direction of Othello's departure), Emilia's ten lines to herself allowing for it. "Dangerous conceits . . ."—the repeated "poisons" may even point to an elision, the gap somewhat awkwardly closed. The sentence itself sums up Iago's scheming; and promptly with that "act upon the blood. . . ." Othello reappears, by the very look of him to warrant the word.[22] Iago's elated, gratified

> I did say so:
> Look, where he comes!

both rounds off this interlude and begins the second encounter between the two.

ANOTHER OTHELLO

Othello's silence as he stands there gains import from the sultrily ominous music of Iago's commenting

himself steals the handkerchief. In the play, to involve Emilia in the matter, she is let find it and hand it to Iago. That is a halfway step to accident, but no more. Nor does the business determine the catastrophe, only helps it on. Accident may find a place, then, in tragedy, as it does in tragic life. But it had better not be pure accident, nor a decisive place.

[22] It is to be noted that the Folio puts Othello's entrance after "I did say so," thus separating this from "Look, where he comes," to avoid which (apparently) modern editors are apt to put it after *that*. But both the Quartos squeeze their stage direction into the margin at "blood." One must not attach too much importance to such things nor found serious argument upon what may be a printer's vagary. But clearly, for the effect of Iago's "I did say so," Othello should, a brief moment earlier, have appeared upon the (inner?) stage.

Not poppy, nor mandragora,
Nor all the drowsy syrups of the world,
Shall ever medicine thee to that sweet sleep
Which thou ow'dst yesterday.

Then, as he paces forward, to that bated

Ha, ha! false to me?

the jaunty

Why, how now, general! No more of that.

is as the setting of a match.[28]

Iago's frigid sapience, those mocking precepts for the complaisant cuckold, are now flung back at him, translated into the agony of

I swear 'tis better to be much abused
Than but to know't a little. . . .
What sense had I of her stolen hours of lust? . . .
I found not Cassio's kisses on her lips. . . .
I had been happy, if the general camp,
Pioneers and all, had tasted her sweet body,
So I had nothing known.

—an agony which obliterates all else, all but itself and the moment, for us, if we feel with him, as for Othello; a factor of import, then, in the action's treatment of time.

But before he yields to his fury, Othello, in terms of what has been noblest to him in life, of

the plumed troop and the big wars
That make ambition virtue! . . .

takes tragic leave of what is noblest in himself. An instant later Iago's ironic concern is shocked into reality when the "waked wrath" of

Villain, be sure thou prove my love a whore. . . .

is loosed first of all upon him.

[28] The Quartos have a reiterated

false to me, to me?

The second "to me" may well be an actor's interpolation; there are, seemingly, a number of them in the play. Even so, it is some slight evidence—any being needed—that the line is meant to be throttled down in the speaking, not rung out clear.

The sudden physical retaliation upon Iago is instinctive; he is not the author only, but the very instrument of torture. The cry for proof, even if it can only be of guilt, and for "ocular proof," is for some actuality which will displace these nightmare imaginings before they riot into madness. The adjuration to Iago to

> abandon all remorse;
> On horror's head horrors accumulate;
> Do deeds to make heaven weep, all earth amazed. . . .

reflects a vision of the abyss into which, if the thing is true, he sees that he himself may fall.

He has, it is evident, his man by the throat; and it is here that, for the first time, Othello loses self-control. Nor is it only that the old quiet authority of

> Keep up your bright swords, for the dew will rust them.

has gone; the later warning to the night-brawlers:

> Now, by heaven,
> My blood begins my safer guides to rule. . . .
> if I once stir,
> Or do but lift this arm . . .

could never have issued in trumpery violence such as this. Iago is stripping him of self-respect. When he next lifts his arm it will be to strike Desdemona.

This futile violence brings no relief, a moment's exhaustion only, which lets Iago recover his jolted wits, and turn his incessantly belauded honesty to good account. An indignant protest—

> Take note, take note, O world,
> To be direct and honest is not safe.
> I thank you for this profit. . . .

—and a dignified essay at departure; and the ashamed Othello will certainly recall him. He remorsefully does; and by that will deliver himself yet more helplessly into his hands, faith in Desdemona wrecked, and none but the wrecker left for guide.

Here is, as it were, the end of one paroxysm of fever. Pending another, we see still at work the infection of mind in which the trouble was begun—

By the world,
I think my wife be honest, and think she is not;
I think that thou art just, and think thou art not. . . .

—at work now upon a weakened nature. Iago can safely administer more violent doses of poison:

You would be satisfied?
Would! nay, I will.
And may: but how? how satisfied, my lord?
Would you, the supervisor, grossly gape on—
Behold her tupped?

and the racked cry of

Death and damnation!

may compensate him somewhat for the indignity of his recent throttling. But the pure pleasure of inflicting pain so intoxicates him that for a second or two he is at a loss:

What then? how then?
What shall I say? Where's satisfaction?

And had Othello still sane eyes to see and ears to hear, the malicious savagery in the

Damn them, then,
If ever mortal eyes do see them bolster
More than their own! . . .
Were they as prime as goats, as hot as monkeys,
As salt as wolves in pride . . .

could not but show him the man. Instead, himself bereft of reason, he demands

a living reason she's disloyal.

and receives instead, in even grosser picturing, only more fuel for his frenzied imaginings; and for "proof"—Iago deftly foisting in the word—a trivial tale of a handkerchief. And this the bankrupt mind welcomes with a pitiful

Now do I see 'tis true.

The essential work is done. And now, in a kind of antiphon to that farewell to the old Othello, is dreadfully conjured up a new:

Look here, Iago;
All my fond love thus do I blow to heaven:
'Tis gone.

> Arise, black vengeance, from thy hollow cell!
> Yield up, O love, thy crown and hearted throne
> To tyrannous hate! Swell, bosom, with thy fraught,
> For 'tis of aspics' tongues! . . .
> O, blood, blood, blood!

In it he blasphemes his so prized Christian baptism, kneeling

> In the due reverence of a sacred vow . . .

to call upon a "marble heaven" to consecrate his revenge. Iago is equal to the occasion, falling upon his knees also, with magnificently histrionic irony, to partake this sacrament of evil, mocking its pagan piety the while. For by his practical doctrine evil is a servant, not a god, and the "wronged Othello's service" of his oath, his own.

> Let him command,
> And to obey shall be in me remorse,
> What bloody business ever.

"Command," "obey"; he can afford to put it so; and note the enticing reminder of the "bloody business." It is in cold blood that one part of the looked-for command is given—

> Within these three days let me hear thee say
> That Cassio's not alive.

—and in covert delight received—

> My friend is dead; 'tis done at your request. . . .

—you rid me, that is to say, of *my* rival and *your* friend. And with this profit on his investment in villainy Iago might wisely be content. But he has grown avid of evil for its own sake; and shall the splendidly lethal force that Othello is, now docile to his hand, be checked here? For a moment he fears so; until his feline

> But let her live.

brings him the assurance of

> Damn her, lewd minx! O, damn her!
> Come, go with me apart; I will withdraw,
> To furnish me with some swift means of death
> For the fair devil.

—suggesting, for the scene's end and its actors' *exeunt*, intents too terrible to be published to this light of day. Finally, two pregnant strokes:

Now are thou my lieutenant.
I am your own for ever.

Iago has won what he set out to win and more; and the double tongue, in that "I am your own. . . ." through which so clearly rings an exultant "You are mine," proclaims the triumph of his double-dealing. But evil has him toiled as fast as he has toiled Othello, and he will trip and fall in the nets of his own weaving.

THE HANDKERCHIEF AGAIN

Enter Desdemona, Emilia and the Clown.

After the prolonged and close-knit tension some such unqualified relief as the Clown now brings with his antic chatter will be welcome. Twenty lines of it encase besides Desdemona's unconsciously ironic message to Cassio:

> Seek him, bid him come hither; tell him I have moved my lord in his behalf and hope all will be well.

Ten more give us her vexation at the mislaying of the handkerchief, and Emilia's underling's face-saving fib about it.[24]

Othello reappears. His head had been aching when she came to fetch him to dinner; hence her

How is't with you, my lord?

He surveys her in enigmatic silence for a moment. To an unexpected tang of the sardonic in his answering

Well, my good lady. . . .
How do you, Desdemona?

she opposes—as if they were well used so to rallying each other—the gently bantering mimicry of her

Well, my good lord.

[24] The concluding

but my noble Moor
Is true of mind and made of no such baseness
As jealous creatures are. . . .

may seem, in critical cold blood, to be too immediately and pointedly apposite for likelihood. But in this it is, in its own way, of a piece with the general compression of the action; and its likelihood passes unquestioned with the rest.

He has his fury on the curb now, but still he finds it "hardness to dissemble," and he approaches this test of the handkerchief fumblingly; at best his forthright nature is not apt at such wiles.

Give me your hand. . . .

—it is actually as if the mind, clogged with inhibited rage, could get no further than the first syllable of the wanted word and thought. Her hand responsively in his stirs the old love and new hate mingled in him to queer sardonic figurings. Her innocent incomprehension leads him to the dead end of a sententious

The hearts of old gave hands;
But our new heraldry is hands, not hearts.

but only for the effrontery—what else!—of her

I have sent to bid Cassio come speak with you.

to spur him promptly to a starting point:

I have a salt and sorry rheum offends me;
Lend me thy handkerchief

—crude, commonplace, all but comic.

Here, my lord.
That which I gave you.
I have it not about me.

She is vexed that she has not; yet for her it is but a handkerchief, to be sought for and sometime found. For him, fury seething in him, imagination luridly aglow, its loss becomes the very emblem of her guilt. And she can call—can she?—his anguished accusations

a trick to put me from my suit . . .

—her brazen suit that Cassio "be received again," which she can urge too by lovingly reproaching him with an

In sooth, you are to blame.

Lest he lose all power of dissembling and kill her then and there, he shakes her off and goes.

This scene is basically cast, and it must be acted, in a key of workaday domesticity[25]; and Desdemona's share of it, more

[25] May not the whole play, indeed, be labeled a "domestic tragedy," Shakespeare's single essay of the kind?

particularly, should be viewed from that standpoint. It is noticeably detached, moreover, in tone and by an incidental touch or so, from yesterday's arrival and the swifter march of the action. Here they are, outwardly, as any comparable couple, married and settled, might be. Witness the knowing Emilia's comment on his outburst of ill-temper:

> 'Tis not a year or two shows us a man.

Desdemona's bewildered

> I ne'er saw this before.

and her later, chastened

> Nay, we must think men are not gods,
> Nor of them look for such observancy
> As fits the bridal.

She is more than vexed at the handkerchief's mislaying. But mislaying is not loss; and he is unwell, and she will not vex him needlessly. Besides, he is otherwise troubled already. Not until later, regretting even her mild part in their squabble—the milder, though, the more exasperating!—does she argue that

> Something sure of state . . .
> Hath puddled his clear spirit; and in such cases
> Men's natures wrangle with inferior things
> Though great ones are their object.

by when, truly, she is, on reflection, puzzled and troubled enough herself to be searching for reassurance.

Was it singularly obtuse of her not at once to detect some menace in that queer scrutiny of her hand and queerer discourse? Here is, indeed, some light upon a factor in her character which contributes, if but passively, to her undoing. Desdemona is utterly unself-conscious. Othello's love for her, moreover, and hers for him, are a part now, she feels, of the natural order of things. They are in the air she breathes. She is uncalculating too, and it belongs to her happiness to be so. For her, with him, to think is to speak; and for him, with her, if the matter concerns the two of them, surely it must be the same. Whatever, then, may be behind his cryptic talk and conduct she will not readily imagine herself to be concerned. Nor in wifely wisdom, if she is not, will she aggravate an ill mood, whether by ignorantly probing or coldly disregarding it. She responds to its equivocal play with banter, with serious simplicity, lastly with a lightly impatient

I cannot speak of this.

—and proceeds to speak of Cassio.

Her suicidal persistence in pleading for him can be put to the account of her uncalculating candor too, of the frankness which is so flawless that, by Iago's evil logic, it may equally be flawless deceit. And here, when for once it is not quite single-minded, bad is made worse, not better.

For Cassio and the handkerchief become gages in a domestic tourney.

> That handkerchief
> Did an Egyptian to my mother give. . . .
> she dying gave it me,
> And bid me, when my fate would have me wive,
> To give it her. . . .
> there's magic in the web of it:
> A sibyl, that had numbered in the world
> The sun to course two hundred compasses,
> In her prophetic fury sewed the work. . . .

—beneath the vehemence of this, of these mordant refrains from the tales of the days of his wooing that she had found so "passing strange," she flinches for a moment; it troubling her too, since the matter seems so to trouble him, that she has tripped into telling him a little less than the truth. But she recovers as quickly. She is no longer that wondering girl, nor a bride even, but a wife confirmed in her status. The handkerchief is precious; but against this extravagant intimidation Venetian dignity and civilized good sense protest in a quietly admonishing

> Why do you speak so startingly and rash? . . .
> Heaven bless us! . . .
> It is not lost; but what an if it were?

And if unhappily it prove to be, he may the better learn that when he is calm. But his peremptory

Fetch't, let me see it.

mere self-respect demands she face with a firm

Why, so I can, sir, but I will not now.

Then, suddenly, she makes the matter a trial of strength between them. Which is to prevail, reason or unreason?—with Cassio's case most unhappily chosen for an example of the reason he must show her.

> You'll never meet a more sufficient man.
> The handkerchief!
>   I pray, talk me of Cassio.
> The handkerchief!
>   A man that, all his time,
> Hath founded his good fortunes on your love;
> Shared dangers with you,—
> The handkerchief!
>   In sooth, you are to blame.

She would soften the reproof by a caress, but with an enraged "Away!" he flings her off and is gone; hers, thus, the immediate victory, yet an ill one to win.

Emilia has some warrant for her sarcastic

> Is not this man jealous?

And if her conscience as she listened has been reproaching her for her own plain lie, her guiltier silence, Desdemona's well-meant evasions may have helped to ease it. A wife may excusably do as much to please a "wayward" husband as to placate an angry one, and a maid be less scrupulous than her mistress. But Desdemona, who asks no such petty victories, stays puzzled and troubled to the point that, Cassio now appearing with Iago, she quite forgets she has sent for him.[26]

She welcomes the distraction, and her generous mind recovers poise in her real concern for "thrice-gentle Cassio's" trouble. Iago deflects her from the thought that after all Othello's anger may somehow have its aim in her.

> Can he be angry?
> Something of moment, then: I will go meet him. . . .

—for, while all is working well, explanations must be prevented.

[26] This will be the normal implication of

> How, now, good Cassio! what's the news with you?

But it is as possible that Shakespeare himself either momentarily forgot it, or—as is more likely—thought it more effective for Iago to bring him to her.

It is this that she modestly and magnanimously enlarges into the

> Something sure of state,
> Either from Venice or some unhatched practice
> Made demonstrable here in Cyprus to him . . .

as sufficient cause. So, without heed to Emilia's coarser wisdom and its warning, she will go seek him too and—"If I do find him fit . . ."—yet again plead Cassio's cause; by which time, in any case, Iago will have him safely out of the way.

She will now be absent from the action for a while, and the fine spirit she brings to it very markedly absent. But this short quiet passage, which is so expressive of her—selfless, high-minded, reasonable of heart—leaves her vivid to remembrance.

Promptly upon her going, and in sharp unlikeness to her, appears the little trull Bianca, the very woman that Iago is persuading Othello—his folly illuminated by the contrast—to believe Desdemona to be.[27] Her affectations find full display in the stale artifice of her

> Save you, friend Cassio! . . .
> What, keep a week away? seven days and nights?
> Eight score eight hours? and lovers' absent hours,
> More tedious than the dial eight score times!
> O weary reckoning![28]

And in the squabble over the handkerchief, travesty of the one just past, we have jealousy reduced to its rightly ridiculous stature.

---

27 Bianca's appearance here illustrates an indefiniteness of place which fits well with uncertainty in time. The handkerchief has been lost somewhere within the bounds of Othello's dwelling. We are still upon that spot. What is Bianca, of all people, doing there? Cassio's surprised and irritated

> What make you from home?

goes halfway—the negative half—to counter the unlikelihood. As to time; he has been—this is explicit—"a week away" from her. Yesterday's landing, then, has quite gone by the board.

28 "Stale artifice" as she will utter it, coming when and where it does, and by contrast with the rest of the verse. Shakespeare could make the same sort of thing sound fresh enough in *Romeo and Juliet* and *A Midsummer Night's Dream*, when the play itself is dominantly cast in the mold of such artifice; and he gives it excellent comic effect in the later *As You Like It*. But here the imagery will sound, as it is meant to, flat and false. And so will Cassio's strained apology in the same kind.

OTHELLO AT IAGO'S FEET

For the next scene's opening Bianca's pretty clinging to Cassio is succeeded by an Iago fastened to the heels of his wounded victim, so to say, and aggravating the wounds:

> Will you think so?
> Think so, Iago?

—the infected mind, under ceaseless sapping, is near exhaustion. Of argument there is no more need; the gross image will serve:

> To kiss in private? . . .
> Or to be naked with her friend a-bed
> An hour or more. . . ?

And the trumpery of the handkerchief—the word, once again, iterated in his ear; Othello, with a feeble snatch at salvation, exclaiming,

> By heaven, I would most gladly have forgot it.

—is now to be turned to conclusive account. Each fresh stroke makes for the man's deeper debasing; and he welcomes them, asks for them:

> Hath he said anything?
> He hath, my lord. . . .
> What hath he said?
> Faith, that he did—I know not what he did.
> What? what?
> Lie—
> With her?
> With her, on her; what you will.

—at which point he physically gives way, and collapses, babbling, *in a trance*, at Iago's feet.

It is a spectacular triumph. The humiliated Ancient has brought his General to this; the dignity, nobility, authority dissolved in these mere debris of a man. He must enjoy it for a moment, cannot but laud his venomous achievement with the ironic

> Work on,
> My medicine, work!

before he turns to a businesslike recovering—for further torture—of the stricken creature.[29]

Cassio appears (told by Desdemona to "walk hereabouts"); but after letting him show his concern Iago finds pretext to be rid of him. The sudden "No, forbear," betokens some fresh plan; and behind the smooth façade of

> The lethargy must have his quiet course. . . .
> Do you withdraw yourself a little while,
> He will recover straight: when he is gone
> I would on great occasion speak with you.

we may divine his brain at work on it.

Cassio gone, Othello recovering, he probably—if surprisingly!—does not intend his opening

> How is it, general? have you not hurt your head?

to bear the scabrous meaning, which the still staggering and obsessed brain, by the reproachful

> Dost *thou* mock me?

so pitifully lends to it. He will be the more amused to note how compulsively his medicine does work. He will note too that, as if from sheer exhaustion, Othello's rage seems to be flagging, since the cynical compliments, which he next metes out to him upon the certainty of his cuckoldom, rouse him to no more than a weary

> O, thou art wise, 'tis certain.

The fresh trick he has now prepared, with Cassio once more for instrument and supplementary victim, will come the timelier, therefore. It is the most puerile of tricks: to provoke Cassio to talk scurril of Bianca and make the listening Othello believe it is of Desdemona. But Iago, grown foolhardy with success, begins now to jerk his puppets with contemptuous ease. He sets his ambush. Cassio will doubtless prove ready game, and he instructs Othello as assiduously as he might a child—who, indeed, cannot resist a preliminary peep from his hiding-place to whisper a

[29] Actors of Iago are accustomed to put their foot, for a moment, upon the prostrate body, even to give it a slight, contemptuous kick. This is wholly appropriate.

Dost thou hear, Iago?
I will be found most cunning in my patience;
But—dost thou hear?—most bloody.

In this passage to come Othello is brought to the very depth of indignity. Collapsed at Iago's feet, there was still at least a touch of the tragic in him, much of the pitiful. But to recover from that only to turn eavesdropper, to be craning his neck, straining his ears, dodging his black face back and forth like a figure in a farce—was ever tragic hero treated thus?[80]

Iago plays his game coolly and steadily, following his own good advice to "keep time in all," giving himself, however, the passing pleasure of pricking Cassio with a

How do you now, lieutenant?

—the wounding word so seemingly needless a slip! He tantalizes the hidden Othello for a while with disconnected phrases and enigmatic laughter, which will make, besides, what he later does let him hear the easier to misinterpret. Bianca's unlooked-for return might well upset his calculations. But by good luck she has the handkerchief itself to fling back at Cassio with the most opportune

A likely piece of work, that you should find it in your chamber, and not know who left it there! This is some minx's token, and I must take out the work? There—give it to your hobby-horse. . . .

and her railing departure lets him send Cassio after her and so be rid of him, his unconscious part in the game satisfactorily played out.

Othello emerges, one thought predominant:

How shall I murder him, Iago?

He would have Cassio "nine years a-killing"; the "noble Moor"

[80] Most actors of Othello, I think, have shirked this scene, wholly or in part; and Salvini (by the note in the Furness Variorum) justified its omission "on the ground that it is not in accord with Othello's character," that it belittled a man of such "haughty and violent temper," was not, in other words—we may fairly gather—in accord with Salvini's own dignity either. But that is, of course, the very point of it. From the dignity of the play's beginning Othello sinks to this, to rise again to the tragic dignity of its end.

The dodging in and out of hiding and the rest of the painfully grotesque pantomime is, of course, the most striking feature of the scene.

is stripped to savagery indeed. Desdemona must be kept in the current of his fury. Iago finds fresh obloquy for her; to be despised by her very paramour:

> And did you see the handkerchief? . . . to see how he prizes the foolish woman your wife! She gave it him, and he hath given it his whore.

He need not fear for her fate:

> A fine woman! a fair woman! a sweet woman! . . . let her rot, and perish, and be damned to-night.

Nevertheless from this moment Othello's torture becomes self-torture too. And the suffering that asks vengeance and the suffering that breeds pity are at intricate war in him, rending him:

> my heart is turned to stone: I strike it, and it hurts my hand. O, the world hath not a sweeter creature. . . . Hang her! . . . but yet the pity of it, Iago! O, Iago, the pity of it, Iago! . . . I will chop her into messes. Cuckold me!

—his nature shown naked to us; no convention of verse or set prose intervening.

Pity, it would seem, might at least so far win as to open a way to the truth, were not Iago there, at his coolest, to steer, by occasional deft touches to the rudder, through this vortex. What smarter goad to a betrayed husband than the derisive

> If you are so fond of her iniquity, give her patent to offend; for if it touch not you, it comes near nobody.

which does, in fact, move Othello to his ultimate

> Get me some poison, Iago; this night. I'll not expostulate with her, lest her body and beauty unprovide my mind again: this night, Iago.[81]

[81] Having spun out *time,* for the sake of likelihood, Shakespeare now accelerates the *action* of the play; the distinction is to be noted. Cassio was to be dispatched "within these three days," while for Desdemona we have had so far nothing more precise than Othello's

> I will withdraw,
> To furnish me with some swift means of death
> For the fair devil.

which followed hard upon Cassio's sentence. Now Desdemona is to die "this night," and Iago promptly promises news of Cassio's death "by midnight." The effect is that of the quickening flow of a river as it enters a gorge and nears a

—for he cannot sustain these agonies longer. But Iago, though poisoning would be the safer plan, has a more pleasing picture in his eye: of Othello destroying with his own hands the beauty he has adored. How fittingly!

> Do it not with poison. Strangle her in her bed, even the bed she hath contaminated.

And Othello, not wicked at heart, yet with a wicked deed to do, snatches, as men will, at whatever vindication:

> Good, good! The justice of it pleases: very good!

the prospect of Cassio's death besides drawing from him an

> Excellent good!

And upon this a trumpet sounds, and Desdemona appears with Lodovico, on embassy from Venice, ceremoniously attended.

By just such a trumpet call was Othello's own happy advent to Cyprus heralded, and we have heard none since. The scheme for his undoing was barely shapen then. This one finds him a man betrayed and self-betrayed, in moral ruin, Iago's creature, sworn to the murder of wife and friend. Yet at the sound, and the symbolic sight in Lodovico of Venice and her sovereignty, he becomes on the instant, to all seeming, the calm and valiant Moor again—frail though the seeming is too soon to prove. It is one of the salient moments of the play, and Shakespeare thus throws it vividly and arrestingly into relief.[32]

---

cataract; our interest quickens as we watch. No inconsistency is involved. That Othello, to be quit of the intolerable strain, and Iago lest his deceit be discovered, should each grow eager to precipitate the catastrophe accords both with circumstance and character.

[32] Modern editions slightly obscure the intended effect by postponing the entrance of Lodovico and Desdemona until Iago has seen them and announced them to Othello, and so given him a second or two in which to recover his equanimity. But Q1 (commonly accepted here also for the spoken text in preference to the Folio) has

> *Ia.* . . . you shall heare more by midnight.
> *A Trumpet.*
> *Enter Lodovico, Desdemona, and Attendants.*
> *Oth.* Excellent good:
> What Trumpet is that same?

The sound of the trumpet and the simultaneous (or all but) entrance of Lodovico and Desdemona will thus surprise him in the very midst of his exulting over the murders to be done, and his effort to control himself will be given its full pictorial value.

Parenthesis: The Use of Lodovico: The Action Advancing of Its Own Momentum

WITH Lodovico's arrival the play enters a penultimate phase, worth brief consideration as a whole; of suspense, enriching of character, of full preparation for the long last scene. The horror of this has already been projected for us in the

> Get me some poison, Iago; this night. . . . Do it not with poison. Strangle her in her bed. . . . Good, good! . . .

and a lesser dramatist, bent on little else, might have cared merely to forge ahead to its consummation, tying off the main threads of the story as best he could by the way. Shakespeare, for all that he is now speeding the action to its end, is in no such haste.

Lodovico's coming weaves a fresh strand into the texture of the play. His mission, the recall to Venice, Cassio's succession—these are weighty matters; and he, bearing the mandate for them, is a figure of consequence. Despite the dire events in prospect then—Othello's murderous passion already breaking surface; Desdemona, vilely outraged, a woman in a daze—due ceremony must still be observed, the customary courtesies offered and accepted, cheerfully withal. Othello knows, the watchful Iago too, and we know, within how short a while the deeds to be done will savagely wreck this fine pattern of procedure. Meanwhile—life, as ordained, must go on.

But for the killing of Cassio—a bagatelle!—Iago's work is done. Until now we have been incessantly conscious of him urging events onward. Now, merely giving them an occasional deft touch or two, he can detachedly observe them, moving to their inevitable end. He comments regretfully—yet not hopelessly—upon their unhappy drift. It is an even more sinister aspect of him. He is pricked to activity again by the sudden reirruption of the absurd Roderigo, by the bringing home to him that he himself, even he, is lapsing into danger—and from such a quarter! He baits the fellow's death-trap with deliberate, economical care; it shall serve for Cassio's also. It is a deadlier, double-edged counterpart to the trick which undid Cassio before. It miscarries. Deprived for the first time of a cat's-paw, Iago has to handle the job himself, and he bungles it.[38] His own undoing has begun.

Thirdly, there is the so-called "brothel scene" and that of the "Willow Song." These are not necessary to the action at all; they are there to illuminate character. The first redresses a much-disturbed balance, and restores to us an Othello who is neither mere bloodthirsty monster nor degraded puppet. The second brings us unforgettably near to a Desdemona defeated in "fortune" but not in goodness, and for the last time fully herself. The play would be impoverished indeed by the loss of these closing episodes of suffering and submission.

Analysis of the Action, Resumed

OTHELLO STRIKES DESDEMONA

By Lodovico's ceremonious salutation, Othello's as ceremonious response—

> God save you, worthy general.
>
> With all my heart, sir.
>
> The duke and senators of Venice greet you.
>
> I kiss the instrument of their pleasures.

(but note the oriental turn of phrase, a touch in it even of ironic humility)—the scene is set moving again upon a seemingly even keel. But beneath the compelled calm his rage will be surging only the more fiercely, we know. So does Iago, retired into watchful silence after his sardonically oracular reply to Lodovico's passing

> How does Lieutenant Cassio?

the

> Lives, sir.

—for another hour or so.

Against this morbid calm—how like, how different from, the quiet dignity of our earliest sight of him—sounds out the happy melody of Desdemona's welcome to her "good cousin Lodovico," token of Venice and home to her, who "shall make all well," who, even better, comes to recall them from the exile to which

[38] It turns out that he has not even, as he supposes, rid himself of Roderigo.

she had so devotedly set out. Her innocently persistent "love I bear to Cassio" wrings from him a stifled

Fire and brimstone!

while its contradiction in her joy at their return—Cassio to be left behind—he only ignores. For he is past reasoning; she besides as likely now to play the whore in Venice as here. His brain, indeed, racked by its efforts at self-control, seems near turning. His speech, when Desdemona nears him, degenerates to a jabbered

I am glad to see you mad.

and upon her ruthful

Why, sweet Othello?

he strikes her.

She does not cry out. And this, with the amazed silence of the rest there, sets a seal upon the atrocious thing. Her only protest:

I have not deserved this.

—then she weeps silently.

Lodovico's grave amazement shows in measured reprobation. But Othello, the blow struck, vindicates it—

O, devil, devil!
If that the earth could teem with women's tears,
Each drop she falls would prove a crocodile.
Out of my sight!

—and augments it with the cold cruelty of

What would you with her, sir? . . .
Ay; you did wish that I would make her turn:
Sir, she can turn, and turn, and yet go on,
And turn again; and she can weep, sir, weep;
And she's obedient, as you say, obedient,
Very obedient. Proceed you in your tears.

He comes, in this zest to insult and degrade her before the world, never nearer in spirit to the "demi-devil" who has ensnared him.

But the violent oscillation of thought begins again. As before between pity and rage, so now between the poles of

Concerning this, sir—O, well-painted passion!
I am commanded home. Get you away;
I'll send for you anon. Sir, I obey the mandate,

And will return to Venice—Hence, avaunt!
Cassio shall have my place. . . .

he sways, until—Desdemona dismissed—as if clutching for very sanity at anything of use and wont, he steadies to a

And, sir, to-night,
I do entreat that we may sup together;
You are welcome, sir, to Cyprus. . . .

and, after a final outburst (lunatic to his hearers; only we and Iago catch the connection):

Goats and monkeys!

follows her.[34]

This long scene, with its fit of epilepsy, with Othello's degradation to eavesdropping and bloodthirsty savagery, with the outrage upon Desdemona, has been the play's most brutal and harrowing yet. It now ends with a quiet, gentlemanly colloquy between Lodovico and Iago; the one so shocked, disillusioned, grieved:

Is this the noble Moor, whom our full Senate
Call all in all sufficient? Is this the nature
Whom passion could not shake? . . .

—the other so regretfully making the worst of it:

He is much changed. . . .
What he might be—if what he might he is not—
I would to heaven he were! . . .
Alas, alas!
It is not honesty in me to speak
What I have seen and known.

Two men of the world, deploring such behavior. But what more—in a difference too between husband and wife—what more than deplore it can they do?

[34] But *do* we, across five hundred lines of speaking time, catch the connection with Iago's

Were they as prime as goats, as hot as monkeys . . .

Not, it is possible, very exactly. But the phrase is a memorable one, and Othello's remembrance of it may sufficiently stir our own. To Lodovico it suggests, with the rest of the wild talk, that he may be off his head. He very nearly is, as the matter of the next scene, to which this phrase is a keynote, will more amply show.

THE "BROTHEL" SCENE: DESDEMONA AT IAGO'S FEET: EMILIA AROUSED

Othello's share in this next scene is, we noted, superfluous to the play's action; yet how impoverished would the picture of him be by the loss of it![35]

He has followed Desdemona. In contrast to the tepid end of the last scene we are admitted into the midst of a sharp cross-examining of Emilia by an Othello whom her pluck, roused for the first time, can at least set twice thinking. But here is the pathos of the matter. This questioning comes too late. He has pledged himself to a besotted belief in Desdemona's guilt. Denial of it now only tortures and enrages him; it is the offer of a comfort he can no longer take, the reminder of a happiness he has lost. Coming from Emilia it is witness to a conspiracy to deceive him; from Desdemona, it only shows her the more hardened in guilt. Committed to his error, he only asks to be sustained in it, and hardened for what he has sworn to do.

So he does his best to shake Emilia's denials, and, when he cannot, relapses upon the sneer of a

That's strange.

—which yet (since his happiness, if lost, is not forgotten) has a tang of wistfulness in it.[36] Whereat Emilia, good fighter that she is, seizes the slight chance:

I dare, my lord, to wager she is honest,
Lay down my soul at stake. . . .

and hammers her daring home, leaving him without retort, but for a conclusive

Bid her come hither. Go.

[35] It is comparable in this respect to the scene in *King Lear* between Lear in his madness and Gloucester in his blindness. By neither is the action advanced; the characters are enriched by both.

[36] The second sentence of his attack on her will read better if it is left a broken one:

Yes, you have seen Cassio and she together—

some opprobrious verb implied, a present participle probably. This will also help to restore the "she" to its nominative, and remove a minor editorial difficulty.

We wait, when he is alone, for some sign that the tide of evil in him may be turning. But all that comes is the

> She says enough; yet she's a simple bawd
> That cannot say as much. This is a subtle whore;
> A closet lock and key of villainous secrets:
> And yet she'll kneel and pray: I ha' seen her do it.

Though he can suffer still and regret, he is too weary-minded now to rid himself of the spell.[37]

Emilia, though unbidden, returns with Desdemona, as if she foresaw danger threatening, and takes her dismissal reluctantly. Then twenty-five words suffice for a vivid prelude to what is to come, and even the action they demand is made plain in them:

> My lord, what is your will?
> Pray, chuck, come hither.
> What is your pleasure?
> Let me see your eyes;
> Look in my face.
> What horrible fancy's this?

—the distantly proud humility of her response to his summons; her approach at his bidding with eyes downcast, since if he feels no shame for the blow struck she feels it for herself and him too; her eyes as obediently lifted, she sees in his for the first time that which appals her.

"I'll not expostulate with her," he had told Iago, "lest her body

[37] It is customary, seemingly, to read this speech as if Emilia were bawd and whore both. But it is Desdemona, surely, whom Othello assails as whore. This is to be the starting point of his coming scene with her. It is certainly her and not Emilia whom he has seen "kneel and pray." Hence the later, sardonic

> Have you prayed to-night, Desdemona?

To gibe at Emilia for praying is sheer dramatic waste.

As to how to identify the

> *This* is a subtle whore. . . .

with Desdemona, that is simple enough. We are momentarily expecting her appearance by the way Emilia has departed. Any competent actor can combine the "this" with a gesture which will unmistakably apply to her.

Let a difficulty be admitted in the

> closet lock and key of villainous secrets . . .

which does seem to connect in thought with the orders to Emilia to "shut the door" and (later) to "turn the key." But Othello's mind is still flinging violently and arbitrarily between one subject and another: and the connection is hardly close or definite enough to invalidate the more dramatically appropriate reading.

and beauty unprovide my mind again. . . ." But he cannot, he finds, forbear. So he first, in self-defense, smirches to himself that "body and beauty" by picturing her as a whore in a bawdyhouse, traded to him for a turn. The sight of her on her knees, looking so "like one of heaven" that the devils themselves might fear to seize her, the very cadence of her protesting

Your wife, my lord, your true and loyal wife.

exclaim against the perversity. He must then needs mesh himself yet deeper in it. Damned once for adultery, she shall "double damn" herself by swearing she is innocent. For her sin against him he will take vengeance. Her sin against herself, her goodness and beauty, and against his faith in them—that breaks his heart. He has only to believe she is innocent when she swears it; but this is the one thing he can no longer do. Nor can he reason and explain; he is as a man hypnotized, possessed. Raised here to the pitch of poetry, it is in substance the commonest of cases. Two beings who have, as have these two, reached intimate communion, cannot, once this is broken, fall back upon a simply reasonable relation.[88] His collapse in tears lets her approach him. She tries to find him excuses for his treatment of her. But what can now bridge the gulf opened between them?[89]

Only slowly has she gathered, does she force herself to understand, what is the "ignorant sin" he will have it she has committed. And not until, emergent from his self-conscious suffering, his eyes on her again, he catches that "committed" with its

[88] Cf. the scene between Hamlet and Ophelia, built upon much the same psychological basis.

[89] What she says of her father here—

if you have lost him,
Why, I have lost him too.

—is not meant to indicate that she already knows of his death. Shakespeare would not let her refer to it thus, "in passing," even at such an otherwise distressed moment as this. We learn of it later, after she is dead herself, from her uncle Gratiano, brought into the action, most inconspicuously, for, it would seem, this sole purpose. Brabantio having been too important a factor in the play to be left unaccounted for at the end. Nor, at this juncture, would Shakespeare want to add a "second string" to Desdemona's suffering. The nearer to the play's end we come, the more important it is to sustain the singleness of the tragic motive. All she means, then, by "I have lost him too" is that (as we know) her father has cast her off.

unlucky connotation of adultery, does he—iterating it, as other words have been set iterating in his hot brain; swinging it round him like a weapon—deal her blow upon blow:

What committed!
Impudent strumpet! . . .
Are not you a strumpet? . . .
What, not a whore?

—blows more grievous by far than that which must physically mark her still. But these she does not take meekly, resists them, rather, with an explicit and religious pride—

No, as I am a Christian:
If to preserve this vessel for my lord
From any other, foul unlawful touch
Be not to be a strumpet, I am none.

—which only drives him back, hardened, upon the brutal sarcasms of his brothel imagery. Resummoning the bewildered Emilia, he leaves her.

Her flash of defiance extinct, she is left spiritually stunned. Her hurt may be measured by the wan humor of her answer to Emilia's troubled question how she does:

Faith, half asleep.

—too deep a hurt for her not to welcome a moment's stupor, not to make light of it, if she but could. She wakes, as out of sleep, to certainty of loss, sees herself in the cold light of it. What is left her but to weep?—and weep she cannot. Sensible to some fatally pending consummation of this inexplicable evil, the dire end to all their joy:

Prithee, to-night
Lay on my bed my wedding sheets: remember. . . .

But she sends too for the shrewd, practical Iago. While she awaits him indignation surges in her

'Tis meet I should be used so, very meet!

—which melts under his velvet touch to the rueful simplicity of

Those that do teach young babes
Do it with gentle means and easy tasks;
He might have chid me so; for, in good faith,
I am a child to chiding.

Nor, a moment later, kneeling there, begging him to intercede for her, is she conscious of any abasement before the two, dependents as they are.

Candor is of the very essence of Desdemona's character, a spontaneous candor, uncalculating, inconsistent; open then to all suspicion. Here what she does and says is as the reflection of passing clouds in a clear mirror. One avowal succeeds another. Each shows her differently, and all with truth.

Childishly, she cannot bring herself to repeat the "name" that Othello has called her. It is at the sound of it, rapped out by the less fastidious Emilia—

He called her whore. . . .

—and upon Iago's so reasonably pertinent enquiry:

Why did he so?

that she at last breaks into tears. Emilia is so filled with wrath and so lost in the satisfaction of venting it, that the solution—

I will be hanged, if some eternal villain,
Some busy and insinuating rogue,
Some cogging, cozening slave, to get some office . . .

—which she hits upon within an inch, still escapes her.

For Iago this is another, and a gratuitous triumph. When Othello fell convulsed at his feet, he had taken pains for that. But to have Desdemona humiliated there too, and imploring his help, is an unlooked for pleasure. He savors it complacently.

The trumpets summon to supper. Desdemona must dry her eyes and once more play the regnant hostess at Othello's side. Iago watches her go, Emilia tending her. Surely he has achieved his end. But he turns to be confronted by an absurdly angry Roderigo.[40]

[40] Another instance of the usefulness of indeterminate locality. Roderigo has not much more business in a room in which Othello and Desdemona have recently been so intimately alone than had Bianca in a similar vicinity. But—unless we are reminded by scenery—we shall not consider this. And the effect to be made here depends upon Iago's sudden turn from his cold survey of the pathetically submissive figure of Desdemona to encounter Roderigo's coxcomb revolt. It would be lost by an exit, a cleared stage, or re-entrance.

RODERIGO AGAIN

Amid these crowding events we may well have—even as it seems for the moment has Iago—all but forgotten his existence; the more comically outrageous, then, the incongruity between Othello's fall, Desdemona's agony and the tale of his own wrongs, into which he so portentously launches:

> I do not find that thou dealest justly with me.

—into the horrors of this pending tragedy thrusts Roderigo, demanding justice!

But we laugh at him unfairly. He knows of no troubles but his own; and there is something pathetic in being so ridiculous in oneself. His case against Iago is strong. He has been most patient. It is time he took a high hand. He has summed up his grievances, sought choice expression for them, studiously—it is evident—rehearsed it, and for once he means to do the talking:

> Every day thou doffest me with some device, Iago; and rather, as it seems to me now, keepest me from all conveniency, than suppliest me with the least advantage of hope. I will indeed no longer endure it. . . .

He finds himself most magnificently overriding Iago's protests. The fellow is his social inferior, after all, and no better than a pimp:

> The jewels you have had from me to deliver to Desdemona would half have corrupted a votarist: you have told me she hath received them and returned me expectations and comforts of sudden respect and acquaintance. . . .

So, despite being tempted into one rather shrilly feeble parenthesis—

> Very well? go to? I cannot go to, man; nor 'tis not very well! . . .

—he reaches his peroration in fine form:

> I will make myself known to Desdemona. If she will return me my jewels I will give over my suit and repent my unlawful solicitation; if not, assure yourself I will seek satisfaction of you.

Iago gives a second or so to the assembling of the implications of this admirable combination of penitence and thrift, and then quickly comments:

You have said now.

—as indeed Roderigo has, and pronounced his own doom.

For the time being there is only Iago's tiger smile to tell us this, although it should suffice. The revealing soliloquy is postponed to a later scene, until the plan now concocting behind the smile shall be actually in action, the ambush set. It will then be speeded through, as at that moment it must be. This both avoids delay here, and denies to the disposing of Roderigo and Cassio the fierce thought given to Othello's ruin. For Iago, flushed with success and scornful of these minor victims, is recklessly improvising now.

But he takes the floor—and the balance of the scene shifts at once—with a magnanimous

> Why, now I see there's mettle in thee; and even from this instant do build on thee a better opinion than ever before. . . .

and overrides Roderigo in turn, and ignores his ill-temper and saps his resolves, and cajoles him and maneuvers him with the old adroitness. Within a little he has the repentant libertine converted to prospective assassin. Yet Roderigo

will hear further reason for this.

Reason and Roderigo go well together.

DESDEMONA DIVESTS HER—FOR DEATH

Between the devising of this first of the midnight murders and its execution we have a scene of ordered calm; of ceremonial courtesy, of Desdemona's divesting her for sleep.

Enter Othello, Lodovico, Desdemona, Emilia and Attendants.

They come from the supper to which we heard the trumpets summon them. It will hardly have been a spontaneously gay repast, as a certain evasiveness in Lodovico's urbane

I do beseech you, sir, trouble yourself no further.

may imply. Each line of these few is lightly pregnant; and an edge to the tone of it, the coloring of the phrase, the actor's look or gesture will tell us what is astir beneath the tension. Othello (it is Emilia's later comment)

looks gentler than he did . . .

—she did not hear, then, his brutal command to Desdemona:

> Get you to bed on the instant; I will be returned forthwith:
> dismiss your attendant there: look it be done.

(the dry anonymity of the "your attendant there" emphasizing their menace) pendant to his as urbane determining of Lodovico's chivalrous courtesy by bowing him on their way together with an undeniable

> O, pardon me; 'twill do me good to walk. . . .
> Will you walk, sir?

So they depart, their escort after them.

In the passage which follows all action whatever, save for the wonted nightly "unpinning," is arrested; there is no other such in the play. Of action of every sort, and of violence and distress of speech, we have so far had plenty. This prepares, in its stillness, and in the gentle melody of the song, for the worse violence and the horror to come, and is, as we have noted, a setting against which no shade of Desdemona's quiet beauty can be lost.

The strain of self-control before Lodovico relaxed, she finds herself suddenly steeped in sheer physical fatigue. She repeats Othello's orders to her—

> He says he will return incontinent:
> He hath commanded me to go to bed,
> And bade me to dismiss you.

—without comment. And her response to Emilia's alert, alarmed

Dismiss me!

is but the listlessly submissive

It was his bidding. . . .

Yet the morose

I would you had never seen him!

draws a quick

> So would not I: my love does so approve him,
> That even his stubbornness, his checks, his frowns, . . .
> have grace and favour in them.

Spiritless? It is not that. But if his love has failed her she must find refuge in her love for him.

Upon her weariness fancies and memories play freely. Reminder of the wedding sheets (imaging—so she had meant them to—the end as the beginning of their wedded joy) begets the fancy to be shrouded in them some day. From that evolves the memory of her dead mother, and of the maid Barbara and *her* "wretched fortune," and the song which "expressed her fortune"; and this recalls Venice, and for Venice stands the handsome, grave Lodovico.

The sad rhythm of the song, as she sings it, soothes her mind, if it leaves her senses still morbidly acute:

> Hark! who is't that knocks?
> It is the wind.

answers matter-of-fact Emilia. And she can note now such petty matters as that her "eyes do itch" and ask lightly if that "doth ... bode weeping," and even half-humorously shake her head over

> these men, these men!

We are seeing the last of Desdemona, but for the midnight moment in which she will wake only to the horror of her death. So, for a finish to the scene, and a completing of her character, Shakespeare stresses the trait in it which has incongruously proved to be the fittest material for this tragedy, the goodness—the too absolute goodness—of a fiber of which Iago's enmeshing net has been made.

It is Brabantio's daughter who now speaks; the daughter of a great house, strictly, isolatingly reared, and conserving—launched into the world—a gently obstinate incredulity of its evil:

> Dost thou in conscience think—tell me, Emilia—
> That there be women do abuse their husbands
> In such gross kind?

and it will be in some incredulity of such innocence that Emilia so circumspectly answers,

> There be some such, no question.

But she is glad of the chance to cheer her mistress with a little salty humor, to agree that "by this heavenly light" she would not wrong her husband, since

I might do't as well in the dark.

and then to treat these tenuous ideals with the hardening alloy of some good coarse common sense. But Desdemona stays unimpressed:

Beshrew me, if I would do such a wrong for the whole world.

and, what is more,

I do not think there is any such woman.

Emilia, her tongue once loosed, waxes eloquent upon wedded life and how to live it. Sound, practical doctrine! Expect little, overlook much; but threaten, and give, tit for tat. And as we listen, and watch Desdemona indifferently listening, and mark the contrast between the two, there may slip into the margin of our minds the thought: better indeed for her had she been made of this coarser clay. But then she would not have been Desdemona.

IAGO BEGINS TO BUNGLE

When Desdemona and Emilia have departed,

Enter Iago and Roderigo.

This is the play's penultimate scene. It is thrown (as usual) into contrast with the quiet colloquy just ended; and the high organic tragedy of the scene to come will in turn stand contrasted with its turmoil. It is besides a counterpart to that other night scene which marked the arrival in Cyprus with Cassio's disgrace, and is thrown into contrast with that too. For while the chief puppets are the same, Iago no longer maneuvers them with the same enjoyable ease; and the stakes in the game are more desperate, no mere thrashing and the cashiering of Cassio, but, by one means or another, death for them both, and quickly, lest puppets turn dangerous. His capital scheme has moved faultlessly towards fruition. But even now what might not happen to stay Othello's hand, or to turn it, or Cassio's, against him? For full success, all the threads must be knotted up and cut together. Well, the "young quat" Roderigo's ire can be turned to the cutting of two at one stroke, since

> whether he kill Cassio,
> Or Cassio him, or each do kill the other,
> Every way makes my game. . . .[41]

He calculates as shrewdly as ever, but more summarily; he plays high and recklessly still. This scene is the last, moreover, of which he directs the action; and its crowding, feverish movement, after the long-sustained scheming, comes as the breaking of a dam. But, ominously, he bungles the stroke which, Roderigo having bungled his, could still rid him of Cassio. By now even *his* nerve is strained. The crisis wrings from him too that strange involuntary

> if Cassio do remain,
> He has a daily beauty in his life
> That makes me ugly. . . .

although, as if surprised by such a thought, he quickly obliterates it beneath the more matter-of-fact

> and, besides, the Moor
> May unfold me to him: there stand I in much peril. . . .

And it is a nakedly brutal scene, in which the first murderous harvest of all the complex trickery and treachery is so summarily reaped.

Ironic flattery of his "good rapier" will not make Roderigo a very competent murderer, but the "satisfying reasons" demanded have at least stiffened that once-sentimental lover to the pitch of a callous

> 'Tis but a man gone.

and a cowardly thrust in the dark. He gets in return yet better than he gives; and, after a few moments groveling agony and one last terrible flash of enlightenment, here will be the end of

[41] The Quartos have "game," the Folio "gaine." The Folio may in general be the better text, but the suggestion of gambling certainly fits the mood of the scene.

him.[42] He has done Iago's schooling some credit; one pities the poor wretch, nevertheless.

Cassio, retaliating on Roderigo, is in turn served out by Iago—who, however, having made no clean job of it, prudently vanishes.[43] The noise brings Othello out upon the balcony above. He has heard Cassio's voice; he knows it well. But in the silence that has fallen and the darkness, his straining ears only catch after a moment Roderigo's low repentant moan:

O, villain that I am!

—a shamefully swift relapse from villainy![44] Cassio's cry, however:

O, help, ho! light! a surgeon!

reassures him—his betrayer dying if not dead—and he exults to the perennial infatuate refrain:

'Tis he. O brave Iago, honest and just,
That has such noble sense of thy friend's wrong!
Thou teachest me. . . .

Up to this moment it has been just possible, we may have felt, that Othello, swinging between rage and suffering, might somehow purge himself of the evil in him. But Iago has set the example, and the wild beast has scented blood:

Minion, your dear lies dead,
And your unblest fate hies: strumpet, I come! . . .

[42] Later it turns out otherwise. We learn in the last scene that

even but now he spake
After long seeming dead. . . .

and witnessed against Iago. But I suspect this to have been an afterthought on Shakespeare's part. In this scene certainly there is no hint that he is not dead, every evidence that he is.

Incidentally Q2 has, when Iago stabs him, *thrusts him in*. The direction implies that there were not (when this edition was viable) two men available to carry away the body at the scene's end, Cassio's chair having the prior claim.

[43] After "But that my coat is better than thou knowest" he does not waste time in thrusting at Cassio's padded doublet, but slashes below it at his groin. Iago's aim would be better and the stroke a fairly fatal one had he not to keep his face hidden. Even so, Cassio can exclaim, "I am maimed for ever. . . . My leg is cut in two!"

[44] Othello's "It is even so" of the Folio, could be read—the voice mistaken for Cassio's—as a savagely sarcastic comment, and perhaps effectively. The Quartos' "Harke, 'tis even so" simply gives continuity to his speech and serves to keep our attention as much upon him as upon the two figures below.

And to the stuttering, choking fury of the crowded last couplet—

> Forth of my heart, those charms, thine eyes, are blotted;
> Thy bed, lust stained, shall with lust's blood be spotted.

—he goes to do the deed prepared. Desdemona is doomed.[45]

As he vanishes Cassio calls out again, and this time Lodovico and the hitherto unknown Gratiano appear.[46] We hear them mistrustfully whispering:

> Two or three groan: it is a heavy night:
> These may be counterfeits: let's think't unsafe
> To come in to the cry without more help.

—and there they stay, and nothing more happens for the moment. Cassio's cries are now reduced to an exhausted "O, help!", Roderigo is still repentantly groaning. Then Iago returns, "in his shirt," like one roused from his lawful slumbers, carrying a light, alert and helpful; just such a ready change worked in him as went with that first swift passing from beneath Brabantio's balcony to the Sagittary, from Roderigo's side to Othello's.

[45] Another passage which producers of the play and actors of Othello conspire to omit, on the ground, presumably, that, as in the eavesdropping upon Cassio, his behavior here lacks dignity. But that, of course, as with the eavesdropping, is the very point of it. In the course of the play Othello is swung, and ever more widely, between the conviction that he is taking righteous vengeance on Desdemona and the primitive savagery which this rouses in him—and without which, it well may be, he could not so overcome his own anguish as to take it. In this stuttering, choking outburst he drops nearer to the savage than ever yet; from it he will have risen, at our next sight of him, to the tragic height of

> It is the cause, it is the cause, my soul. . . .

[46] If the stage for which *Othello* was written boasted not only the center balcony, *i.e.*, the upper stage, but one over each of the side doors as well, I think that almost certainly Lodovico and Gratiano appeared upon one of these. But the center one alone would be wide enough to allow them to enter it by one side an instant after Othello has left it by the other without seeming to be in awkward proximity to him. There is nothing against this in their own

> To come *in* to the cry . . .

or in Iago's appeal

> What are you there? Come *in* and give some help.

the "in" being merely a figure of speech; if it were not, "out" would be the appropriate word. In either case they seem to be meant to respond by descending to the lower stage: and while they pass momentarily out of sight in doing so, Iago can the better dispatch (as he thinks) the wounded Roderigo. He then confronts them below with his

> What may you be? Are you of good or evil?

He seems not to recognize Cassio; how should he look to find him here? When he does his commiseration is heartfelt:

> O me, lieutenant! what villains have done this?

—for he cannot at the moment finish his bungled job, since, he notes, there are onlookers now. But he can at least do swift justice upon the one villain who

> is hereabout
> And cannot make away.

And the prostrate Roderigo is welcome to see his face as he stabs him, for he will take care not to miss his stroke this time. He finds, indeed, some pleasure in thus winding up accounts with his dupe. And he easily drowns the aghast shriek:

> O damned Iago! O inhuman dog!

with a stentorianly indignant

> Kill men i' the dark! Where be these bloody thieves?

Roderigo, he may well suppose, will trouble him no more.[47]

For an instant, as he stands there by the body, nothing stirs.

> How silent is this town!

he says; an accusing silence which he breaks with an echoing

> Ho! murder! murder!

Those prudent onlookers approach—Lodovico he recognizes, the other is less distinguishable—and he can now, with them to witness, give undivided care to Cassio, his stricken comrade, his very "brother"; grief wrings the word from him.

He makes sure that Cassio has no clue to his assailants. Bianca's appearance, and her hysterical collapse at the sight of her lover, offer her to him for a scapegoat. The lifeless Roderigo, recognized and well wept over, may be turned to more account yet.[48] And

---

[47] See, however, p. 72, note 42, and page 94, note 61.

[48] There may be, I think, a textual error here in Iago's repetition of Bianca's

> Who is't that cried?

He can scornfully echo her; I see no other reading, nor very much dramatic point in that. It is possible, therefore, that Iago's original sentence is lost and that this replaces it.

That Shakespeare has every thread here clear in his mind is shown by Gratiano's telling Cassio that he has been to seek him. It will have been to

while he mentally assembles the factors for some fresh, plausible fiction, he is here, there and everywhere, binding Cassio's wound, summoning a chair for him, seeing him safely into it and away. He is as ready and quick as ever; but possibly too quick, somewhat emptily ready. It is easy to browbeat Bianca, and he does so with gusto, arraigning her before these Venetian dignitaries Lodovico and Gratiano:

> Stay you, good gentlemen. Look you pale, mistress?
> Do you perceive the gastness of her eye?
> Nay, if you stare, we shall hear more anon.
> Behold her well; I pray you, look upon her:
> Do you see, gentlemen? Nay, guiltiness will speak,
> Though tongues were out of use.

All very menacing! But of *what* he is to accuse her he has evidently no idea; he is searching as he speaks. Emilia's arrival and the need to repeat the tale to her give him the liar's valued chance to tell the economized truth. He pursues the Bianca trail:

> Prithee, Emilia,
> Go know of Cassio, where he supped to-night.
> What, do you shake at that?

But Bianca, by now, is in fighting trim, and can answer Emilia's

> Fie, fie upon thee, strumpet!

with a smart

> I am no strumpet, but of life as honest
> As you that thus abuse me.

Each boasts and counterboasts her respectability until Iago cuts them short with

> Emilia, run you to the citadel,
> And tell my lord and lady what hath happed.

Another blunder, thus to send her posting off! Might she not

---

inform him of his promotion to governor. Gratiano, who brings also the news of Brabantio's death, is a later arrival from Venice than Lodovico. It is the last of these compressions of the action, and very inconspicuously made. Note besides that while there are several references to the governorship, the last in Cassio's presence at the end of the play, he is never told of it directly. As with Brabantio's death, of which Desdemona is never told, Shakespeare does not want at this juncture to give a subordinate matter primary importance.

come in time to stop the murderous work afoot then? But his final

This is the night
That either makes me, or foredoes me quite.

(he stays behind the rest to confide it to us), with the old confident swagger marred for the first time by a strain of doubt, speaks of some sense in him that his "divinity of hell" may not have armed him quite invincibly after all.[49]

THE END

The events of the first three scenes of the play, we noted, could be presumed to pass in just about the time it took to act them, and this was time enough for an exhibition of the chief characters concerned. Then came a speeding of events and drastic com-

[49] At two points in this scene the question can be raised of the comparative effect to be made by implied as against actually exhibited action.

When Othello departs with that savagely menacing

Strumpet, I come! . . .

to what extent does he leave us thinking of him, as the bustling scene proceeds, on his way to kill Desdemona? The thought, I believe, will persist; because her fate is the capital issue, while the recovery of Cassio and the dispatching of Roderigo, with which the actual action is occupied, are secondary ones. But action exhibited will always command primary attention. This thought of Othello, therefore, will occupy no more than the margin of our minds; it will form a latent, though very living, link with our next expected sight of him.

When Emilia is bid "run . . . to the citadel" and hastens off, the sight, coupled with this latent thought of Othello, may stimulate the question whether she can overtake him, cannot at least arrive in time, even whether (in an alertly minded audience) Iago has not therefore blundered by sending her. But the thought of her on her way will not persist with us as did the thought of Othello on his, if only because the now succeeding action involves Othello and Desdemona themselves and her murder and will obliterate thought of all else. The intended effect, indeed, is that it should. Then, when she knocks at the door we shall recall her hastening off, and the question is stimulated, with the tacit comment: Too late, after all!

But is it legitimate, and is it consistent with Shakespeare's ever most practically minded exercise of his art to provide for these secondary effects, which, it would appear, a given audience may not appreciate, fully or perhaps at all? The answer surely is: yes, as long as they *are* secondary and the primary are neither sacrificed to their success nor will be prejudiced by their abortion. They can be compared to the inner parts of a piece of orchestral music. At a first hearing only an expert may detect them and appreciate their enrichment of the whole. The rest of us may need half a dozen hearings. But the more there is to discover the greater will be the interest; and this can be as true of a play as of music.

pression of time. Now, since Lodovico's coming, the action has been only normally compressed, the scenes strung loosely along, *within* them little or no time-compression; and within this long final scene there is to be none at all. For Othello, indeed—who is never absent from it, upon whom its entire action centers—it is as if, once his sworn deed is done, time and life itself lose all momentum. We have seen him, after one storm, joyfully make port. Here, after another, is the ship slowing—his own imagery—to her "journey's end."

The scene falls into three sections: the first filled by Desdemona's murder, the second by the discovery of Iago's guilt and the killing of Emilia, the third by Othello's orientation to his own end. The murder is soon accomplished, and it is but the consummation of what has gone before. From then until he kills himself he takes little more than a passive share in the action. It eddies about him: but he has lost all purpose, and even the attack upon Iago is half-hearted. Montano (though "puny whipster" he is not) easily gets his sword from him. So the bulk of the scene is given to a survey of the spiritual devastation that has been wrought in him. Bit by bit, the "noble Moor" who was "all in all sufficient," is revealed to himself and the others as a gull, a dolt, "as ignorant as dirt," the "good" Othello as a savage monster; and the soldier, firm and renowned in action, yet guilty of *this* action, is reduced to futile gestures and inarticulate bellowings of remorse. It is a terrible, shameful spectacle, of which Shakespeare spares us nothing, which, indeed, he elaborates and prolongs until the man's death comes as a veritable relief, a happy restoring of him to dignity.

Enter Othello with a light, and Desdemona in her bed.[50]

Of all the contrasts in the play between the end of one scene and the opening of the next, or the disappearing and reappearing of a character, none is more striking than this, than the passing

[50] According to Q2. Q1 also has *with a light*; but the Folio omits it, and editors have, in consequence, preferred to have a light already burning in the room. This is not quite such a small error as it may seem. The intention in Q2 plainly is that Othello shall enter with the light illuminating his face; and the steadiness with which he carries the (presumably) naked candle does much to emphasize the abnormal calm which gives dramatic distinction to his appearance.

from the alarms of Roderigo's murder and Cassio's wounding, from the reciprocal scoldings of Bianca and Emilia, to the sublimity of Desdemona's sleep, and from our last sight of Othello, clothed with fury, lusting for her blood, to his entry here, as a priest might come to do sacrifice, bearing his light, uttering his oracular

> It is the cause, it is the cause, my soul:
> Let me not name it to you, you chaste stars!
> It is the cause.

He is calm as water is when near to boiling, or the sea with a surge of storm beneath. Exalted in his persuasion that it is justice he deals and not vengeance, he regains a satanic semblance of the nobility that was. He had feared "lest her body and beauty" might "unprovide" his mind. The spell of them is working in him, the first cold image of

> that whiter skin of hers than snow
> And smooth as monumental alabaster.

quickening, through vision of the living light beneath, to a full sense of them; this pursued beyond to the charnel

> Be thus when thou art dead, and I will kill thee,
> And love thee after. . . .

—the initial perverting of the mind finding such final issue; as too in the bitter

> I must weep,
> But they are cruel tears. . . .

as in the blasphemy of

> This sorrow's heavenly;
> It strikes where it doth love.

Desdemona wakes; and, as she would at any time—must have, it will seem, so many times—calls drowsily,

> Who's there? Othello?
> Will you come to bed, my lord?

A poignant incongruity: he, wrought and intent, ready to kill; she but slowly shaking free from the sleep which weariness has sent and innocence not denied her, passing, rather, indeed, from sleep to nightmare, to the incredible sight of him with eyes rolling, passion shaking his "very frame," to incredible talk of crime and killing and guilt, until, her heart palsied, she gasps,

> why I should fear I know not,
> Since guiltiness I know not; but yet I feel I fear.

Bewildered, she fences against his fierce

> Think on thy sins.

and threat of death with pretty quibbling conceits—so unreal it all still seems to her—until he beats the futile weapon down with an ultimate

> Peace and be still!

She is awake now and collected, and wifely compliance joins with womanly dignity:

> I will so. What's the matter?

The handkerchief! That this ridiculous trifle should be her death warrant, that her plain provable denial now comes too late to outweigh the "strong conception" of her guilt this madman has been brought to "groan withal"—here the play's tragic irony is sharpened to its keenest point. Add the final instance following, in which wickedness and folly together are able to "turn her virtue into pitch," her peculiar goodness, that uncalculating candor, to her harm. Cassio's death, when she hears of it, means her undoing, since his witness to her innocence will be denied her. It is in innocence that she connects the two:

> My fear interprets then. What, is he dead? . . .
> Alas, he is betrayed, and I undone!

—that blind innocence!—and her tears are a terrified child's. But Othello's distorted mind can only read in it more evidence of her guilt.[51]

[51] "My fear interprets then. . . ." This is the reading of the two Quartos. It contributes to a more regular, and perhaps, therefore, a more authentic line than is the Folio's "O, my fear interprets." (An initial "O," breaking the meter, itself hints at an actor's interpolation.) The meaning is, I take it—though the one reading does not make it clearer than the other, nor either very clear—that her present vivid fear interprets for her at last Othello's bewildering anger at the loss of the handkerchief, the blow, the "impudent strumpet" and the rest. Desdemona's gentle courage has been, throughout the play, a striking feature of her character. It goes with her candor and lack of suspicion, her blindness to the evil enmeshing her.

It is in cold deliberate anger that he kills her. We are spared none of the horror, neither her panic struggles, nor the hangman humanity of his

> Not dead? not yet quite dead?
> I that am cruel am yet merciful;
> I would not have thee linger in thy pain:
> So! So![52]

The abrupt knocking at the door and Emilia's insistent voice can set his wits alertly on the defensive even while the fully sentient man barely yet comprehends what he has done. His

> She's dead. . . .
> Ha! no more moving?
> Still as the grave. . . .
> I think she stirs again. No. . . .

shows a mind working detached—and the more swiftly—within senses still benumbed. It is with the

> If she comes in, she'll sure speak to my wife. . . .

[52] There is a reading hereabouts in Q1, which is now generally rejected but which nevertheless invites comment. The accepted Folio text for the moment of the smothering runs

> *Des.* Kill me to-morrow, let me live to-night.
> *Oth.* Nay, if you strive.
> *Des.* But halfe an houre.
> *Oth.* Being done, there is no pawse.
> *Des.* But while I say one prayer.
> *Oth.* It is too late. *Smothers her.*
> *Ameilia at the doore.*
> *Aemil.* My Lord, my Lord? What hoa?
> My Lord, my Lord . . .

Q1, besides the omission of "Being done, there is no pawse," and such slight changes as to *He stifles her* and *Emillia calls within*, has, after "It is too late,"

> *Des.* O Lord. Lord. Lord.

Since Dyce reproved Collier for admitting this to the edited text (Furness Variorum: footnote, p. 302) on the grounds that the effect involved was, first, "not a little comic" and secondly "disquietingly vulgar," no other editor appears to have raised the question. But it is worth consideration at least. For the effect (saving Dyce's opinion) would at least be neither comic nor vulgar, and might prove to be very poignant indeed. Imagine it: Desdemona's agonized cry to God, and as the sharp sound of it is slowly stifled, Emilia's voice at the door rising through it, using the same words in another sense. A macabre duet, and unaccountable enough to call from Othello a most distraught

> What voice is this? . . .

that he stumbles—the intimate word itself piercing him—into the light of the irrevocable fact; to cry out then in amazed agony:

> My wife! my wife! what wife? I have no wife.

The deed done, the passions so tortuously wrought up to its doing begin to unravel. From the wreck of the Othello that was emerges a man who is both the victim and the creature of the deed.

His grief is as ingenuous as a child's:

> O, insupportable! O, heavy hour!

the man's awed sense of guilt is as unmeasured:

> Methinks it should be now a huge eclipse
> Of sun and moon, and that the affrighted globe
> Should yawn at alteration.

It is a furtive criminal that draws the curtains round the bed to admit Emilia with a bantering

> What's the matter with thee now?

and a callous one that answers her

> O, my good lord, yonder's foul murders done!

with the bland mockery of

> What, now?

And through the somber

> It is the very error of the moon:
> She comes more near the earth than she was wont
> And makes men mad.

speaks a spirit accursed.

The news of Cassio's escape rekindles his fury. It is quenched on the instant by the sound of that voice from the dead:

> O, falsely, falsely murdered!

—Desdemona's; she is in Emilia's arms, faintly proclaiming (as for answer to the horror-struck "O, who hath done this deed?" she gasps out her pitifully preposterous "Nobody; I myself. . . .") *his* guiltlessness too. A last corroboration of her other perjuries, if he will! Then, with the soul-searing

> Commend me to my kind lord. . . .

she is dead indeed.

The man's riven mind seems, for a moment, in the evasive

> Why, how should she be murdered? . . .
> You heard her say yourself, it was not I.

to be self-contemptuously sounding, under Emilia's accusing gaze, the depths of the ignominy of acquittal thus opened for him, to reject it by frenetically, exultantly invoking an eternal vengeance now upon the gentle dead:

> She's like a liar gone to burning hell:
> 'Twas I that killed her.

Whereupon, with volcanic Emilia, it is quick blow for blow, given and taken; from him the foul word to vindicate the brutal deed—

> She turned to folly, and she was a whore. . . .
> Cassio did top her. . . .

—from her plain "devil . . . devil." Yet out of the coarse melee rises his challenging

> O, I were damned beneath all depth in hell,
> But that I did proceed upon just grounds
> To this extremity.

soars too, in anguished remembrance, the ecstatic

> Nay, had she been true,
> If heaven would make me such another world
> Of one entire and perfect chrysolite,
> I'ld not have sold her for it.

It is not however these splendid protests that strike Emilia, but the cursory

> ask thy husband else. . . .
> Thy husband knew it all.

which slips out besides; this leaves her for an instant breathless. Then she finds herself re-echoing, her first stupidly echoed "My husband!" and again, with horror doubled and redoubled, as every echo of it draws from Othello the ever more horrible truth. And she cries to the unhearing dead:

> O, mistress, villainy hath made mocks with love!

Horror comes to a head, and clarifies:

My husband say that she was false?

He, woman:

I say thy husband: dost understand the word?
My friend, thy husband, honest, honest Iago.

Reckless of consequence, she deals a deliberate hammer-blow:

If he say so, may his pernicious soul
Rot half a grain a day! He lies to the heart. . . .

Although Othello, baited and exasperated, the murderous blood still hot in him, draws sword on her now, a choking dread is rising in him. She defies him and his lowering

Peace, you were best.

And it is she who stoutly checks and silences him and holds him there, a culprit, while she vociferates to all who may hear to come and arraign him.

A Parenthesis: The Play's Finishing

THE finishing of the play is technically not a very simple task. There are the customary conventions to fulfill. Iago's treacheries must be disclosed, and not only to Othello; they must be published to the rest of this mimic world also. Such a methodical completing of the story seems on a stage such as Shakespeare's, where illusion is uncertain, to confirm its credibility; it resembles the old-fashioned "proving" of a sum. This outcry from Emilia will assemble everyone concerned. If story were all, the threads could now be combed out and tied up expeditiously enough. But the play is a tragedy of character; and Othello's—even though no spiritual salvation will dawn for him—is not to be left in mere chaos. The dramatist's task, then, is to restore him as much to himself, and to such a consciousness of himself, as will give significance to his end, and to do this convincingly without pursuing the action beyond appropriate bounds.

Consider, for comparison of treatment, other such Shakespearean partnerships in death. Romeo and Juliet die from simple mishap, divided by a few minutes of time; and the completing of the story follows as a long—and rather tiresome—anticlimax. This is early work. *Othello*, *Antony and Cleopatra*, *Macbeth*;

these are all three mature, and in each case the method of the ending fits story and characters appropriately together. Between Antony's death and Cleopatra's, action is interposed that lends hers an importance matching his, even as in life the two are matched; and this can be very suitably done since the scope of the story is so wide. Lady Macbeth, on the other hand, has been reduced, well before the play's end, to the wraith of the "sleep-walking" scene; and she dies actually "offstage." But from the moment of Duncan's murder she has been a slowly dying woman, the battlefield is no place for her; and her death, made much of, might, the action close-packed as it is, inconveniently outshine Macbeth's.

As to Othello and Desdemona; if he is to be restored to dignity his death must not come as an anticlimax to hers. Yet, as in cause, so in effect, it must closely depend on hers. Shakespeare makes, then, no break in the action; and he keeps Desdemona's murdered body the motionless, magnetic center of it, silently eloquent until the end. Again, Othello cannot be let actively dominate the scene until his end is imminent. It would never do, for instance, to have him personally dragging the truth from Iago, Emilia or Cassio, tritely reversing in epitome the process of his deception. To avoid such recapitulation, Iago, before he appears for the second time as a prisoner, has already "part confessed his villainy," and will obstinately refuse to say more, while Cassio will not appear till then, when there is nothing much left for him to say. For a channel of disclosure we have the impetuous Emilia, who herself has it all to learn, for an instrument the handkerchief, which she set on its fatal course. Nor can Othello himself do justice on Iago. As requital for Emilia's death it would be inappropriate; he does not care whether she lives or dies. And to kill him a moment before he kills himself would be a discounting of the effect of his own end. What initiative is left him, then, until the time comes for him to do justice on himself? It follows that the tension of the scene must be sustained for the most part without him. Yet he must never be deprived of his pre-eminent place in it. The dramatic task involved is by no means an easy one.

Analysis of the Action, Concluded

To the Folio's

Enter Montano, Gratiano and Iago.

the Quartos add, *and others*; and there is gain in the sudden irruption of half a dozen or more figures, from among which Emilia picks out, even before we may, the one that counts, with her keen

O, are *you* come, Iago? . . .[53]

Yet he is her husband; and he must clear himself. Desperately she bids him

Speak, for my heart is full.

But her fiery challenging brings instead only sourly evasive admissions, and to the damning

My mistress here lies murdered in her bed. . . .
And your reports have set the murder on.

no answer at all, except (amid the appalled murmurs) for Othello's suddenly weary, strangely empty

Nay, stare not, masters: it is true indeed.

And for a helpless moment it even seems as if, the deed irrevocable, Othello, the man he is, with vengeance on a guilty wife—one woman's voice alone swearing her guiltless—not unpardonable, here might be coming an end to the whole matter.[54]

It is the one woman who will not have it so. While Montano and old Gratiano deplore the thing done, Emilia, with her

Villainy, villainy, villainy! . . .

is flinging herself on the track of the true doer frantically, incoherently flogging her every faculty into use:

I think upon't: I think: I smell't: O villainy!
I thought so then: I'll kill myself for grief:
O villainy, villainy!

[53] The Folio's later speech-heading "*All*" gives countenance to the Quartos' "*and others*," since it can hardly be meant to indicate Montano and Gratiano alone.

[54] It should be noted, however, that Lodovico, the man of authority, is not present.

As cool as she is frantic, Iago marks a danger signal in that "I thought so then . . . ," and he orders her home, out of the way. He will mark another in her stricken

Perchance, Iago, I will ne'er go home.

—since she is ready now for the worst. But Othello's sudden collapse in inarticulate agony takes all eyes and ears, and for the moment she is stayed. His savage rage dissolved in savage grief, she finds relief from her own anguish in the sight of his, a satisfaction even:

Nay, lay thee down and roar;
For thou hast killed the sweetest innocent
That e'er did lift up eye.

And they unite in grief for the dead Desdemona. Even Othello's exculpatory

O, she was foul! . . .

laments her; and in the echoing

'Tis pitiful. . . .

compunction wells again. And Gratiano's gentle

Poor Desdemona! I'm glad thy father's dead. . . .

takes no account of guilt or innocence. He and the rest there stand and gaze.

Only Iago holds frigidly, vigilantly apart, the sight of him so reminding us that where he is evil is brewing still. Then Othello's

but yet Iago knows . . .

turns every eye on him again.

That she with Cassio hath the act of shame
A thousand times committed . . .

—this, with its frenzied "thousand times" raising the scene to fever pitch again—

Cassio confessed it:
And she did gratify his amorous works
With that recognizance and pledge of love
Which I first gave her. . . .

Iago can tell what is coming, and there is no stopping it. He has a wary eye on Emilia—

I saw it in his hand:
It was a handkerchief. . . .

—and, when he sees the light of this break on her, a dangerous one. But there is a deadlier power left in that "trifle light as air"—and a livelier danger to *him*—than he would suppose; witness for response, upon a note she has never sounded till now, Emilia's deep searching

O God! O heavenly God![55]

This handkerchief, then, has been the instrument of Desdemona's death; she the cat's-paw to handle it; her pleasuring of Iago, her petty lie, her silence, all means to the appalling end. And God above has permitted this. What shall she do?

Iago, alert to a fresh force in her, gives her full warning; first with a sharp

Zouns, hold your peace.[56]

(But "'Twill out, 'twill out. . . ." she cries; her strong spirit crying through her); then, after a moment, with a cold and clear

Be wise, and get you home.

And would she be so wrong to be wise? She can no longer mend the matter. What profit therefore now in pinning guilt upon Iago—and he her husband after all? She can read besides in his look what will befall her if she does. She might well choose to be wise. But if she cannot restore Desdemona to life, to honor and

[55] The Q1 reading; the Folio (also, substantially Q2) having

Oh Heaven! oh heavenly Powres!

The difference, at this point, is not a slight one; Q1 striking the far stronger note. It is generally admitted that the text of *Othello* bears many marks of the 1605 "Act against Swearing" (and one has but to glance at the Concordance, with its two entries under "God" and its long list under "heaven"). The line in the Quarto has, therefore, that much inferential claim to be what Shakespeare first wrote. But a more important argument in its favor is its challenging intent, so closely akin to Laertes' "Do you see this, O God?"; to Macduff's "Did heaven look on and would not take their part?" (which should surely read "God," the whole scene hereabouts being enfeebled by repeated "heavens"); and, of course, to more than one passage in *King Lear*—where, however, Shakespeare escapes difficulties with the Censor by expressly "paganizing" the play. But this challenging attitude towards divinely permitted evil is characteristic of the mature tragedies.

[56] Q1 also.

her innocent name she can. Therefore, without need to question what she shall do, she answers that cold, clear "Be wise. . . ." as clearly with a resolute, deliberate

I will not.

—and, for the dead Desdemona's sake, faces her fate.

Then and there Iago draws his sword. It is not the most plausible of ways, this, one would suppose, to confute Emilia. But guile, failing, turns into foul abuse, and "honest Iago" into the trapped beast, fangs bared. To which monster it is that Gratiano makes gentlemanly protest:

Fie!
Your sword upon a woman!

Emilia speaks on. If the words are to be her last she will leave nothing in doubt:

O thou dull Moor! that handkerchief thou speaks't of
I found by fortune and did give my husband. . . .
She give it Cassio! No, alas, I found it,
And I did give't my husband.

—nor minimize (witness the stressed and repeated "my husband") her own blind partnership in the villainy. With all eyes on the two of them, Iago is kept at bay. But when—coming, indeed, like a very clap of it!—the tremendous

Are there no stones in heaven
But what serve for the thunder?

turns attention to Othello, he slips through the defense, wreaks vengeance on her and is gone.

But for kindly old Gratiano, Emilia would fall and die there unheeded; and, after a moment's care of her, even he leaves her for dead. The rest have still only eyes for Othello, whom Iago's escape leaves balked, silenced, motionless, yet with such giant menace in the very look of him that Montano must wrest his sword away, and, General though he be, set drastic guard over him till the fugitive can be caught and justice done. So sentries are set without the door; and they leave him there, disarmed and imprisoned, alone with the dead Desdemona and the dying Emilia.

He sinks into impotence:

I am not valiant neither,
But every puny whipster gets my sword.
But why should honour outlive honesty?
Let it go all.

—into an oblivion which even Emilia's dying words do not pierce. She, dragging herself to Desdemona's side, her mind wandering—back to the refrain, the "Willow, willow, willow," which was her mistress' last sad gift of herself to her—can yet rally strength to take the death-witnessed, never-doubted oath:

Moor, she was chaste; she loved thee, cruel Moor;
So come my soul to bliss, as I speak true;
So speaking as I think, I die, I die.

But it is all unregarded that she dies.

His mind is elsewhere. He says to himself,

I have another weapon in this chamber;
It is a sword of Spain, the ice-brook's temper;
O, here it is. Uncle, I must come forth.

Whereupon he proceeds to play a grimly comic little practical joke upon Gratiano, who is on guard without, armed with the sword Montano had secured. The old man's voice protests confidently:

If thou attempt it, it will cost thee dear;
Thou hast no weapon. . . .

Othello is actually wielding his new-found one as he answers with boyish cunning:

Look in upon me then, and speak with me,
Or, naked as I am, I will assault thee.

And when Gratiano innocently does so, there stands the prisoner, formidably rearmed.[57]

If he meant, as it will seem, to pursue Iago, the impulse is dead in him already. But his soldierly dignity must be retrieved from

[57] A typically Shakespearean device: to follow the tragic moment of Emilia's death by this semi-comic trick, so both separating it from the tragedy still to come, and heightening this by contrast.

that momentarily humiliated depth of "I am not valiant neither . . . ," even if to the

> I have seen the day
> That with this little arm and this good sword
> I have made my way through more impediments
> Than twenty times your stop. . . .

he must now add a bitter

> O, vain boast!

He stands there an awe-inspiring figure still, in outward seeming still the Othello who had but to lift his arm for the best of them to sink in his rebuke. But the fire within is cold, the purpose gone:

> Be not afraid, though you do see me weaponed;
> Here is my journey's end, here is my butt
> And very sea-mark of my utmost sail. . . .

wan echo, this, of the ardent

> O, my soul's joy!
> If after every tempest come such calms . . .

of the whelming

> Like to the Pontic sea,
> Whose icy current and compulsive course . . .

—the mighty and untamable sea that has been throughout the image most consonant to his nature.

Then he turns to the dead Desdemona:

> Now, how dost thou look now?[58]

and takes, with Gratiano for witness (whose grave compassion will exemplify our own as we listen), another and very different farewell of her. The up-wrought

> whiter skin of hers than snow
> And smooth as monumental alabaster.

becomes a simple

> O, ill-starred wench!
> Pale as thy smock!

[58] And he must, I think, pull back the curtains of the bed, and, if need be, raise the body, so that the dead face can be plainly seen.

For his murderer's look which so terrified her we have now

> When we shall meet at compt
> This look of thine will hurl my soul from heaven,
> And fiends will snatch at it.

and, for his mortal assault on her with its "Strumpet . . . strumpet!", the timid touch of his finger on her breast or cheek, and the dull

> Cold, cold, my girl!
> Even like thy chastity.

It is their last communion: her visionless gaze, his unavailing words.

With a quick twist his thoughts pursue Iago:

> O, cursed, cursed slave!

to be flung back upon his own maddening guilt:

> Whip me, ye devils,
> From the possession of this heavenly sight! . . .

(his macabre

> Be thus when thou art dead, and I will kill thee,
> And love thee after. . . .

has ripened into this). It is his last and stormiest fit of such passion

> Blow me about in winds! roast me in sulphur!
> Wash me in steep-down gulfs of liquid fire! . . .

It subsides into the deep, measured diapason of

> O, Desdemona! dead Desdemona: dead!

—the irrevocable indeed in that last word, and in a softly added

> Oh, oh!

dumb suffering and remorse.[59]

[59] The Folio reading. Most editors here follow the Quartos'

> O *Desdemona, Desdemona* dead. O, O, O.

(Q2 replacing Q1's comma after the second "Desdemona" by a semi-colon).

Too much importance must not be attached to minor phrasing or to punctuation, which may in fact be either the prompter's or the printer's. But the Folio reading here happens to be substantially preferable, both in its repetition of "dead" (the added emphasis being of much dramatic value) and for the weightier rhythm and melody, which help to make the line the solemn

In the ensuing silence Lodovico appears, escorted, and embodying once more the majesty of Venice itself. Montano is with him, and behind them is the captured Iago, disarmed and guarded. The wounded Cassio comes too, carried in a chair. And the scene which follows has the semblance of a tribunal, over which Lodovico authoritatively presides.[60]

He addresses the one culprit indirectly, considerately, commiseratingly:

> Where is this rash and most unfortunate man?

and Othello accepts disgrace:

> That's he that was Othello: here I am.

He treats the other as fittingly:

> Where is that viper? bring the villain forth.

and the two are confronted.

Iago is silent, and his face a mask. Hence (at one remove of thought) Othello's baffled

> I look down towards his feet: but that's a fable. . . .

A swift stroke at the pinioned creature—

> If that thou be'st a devil, I cannot kill thee.

---

apostrophe I think it is meant to be instead of giving countenance to yet another mere outcry.

It is interesting to compare this whole passage with that in which Lear apostrophizes the dead Cordelia. We have the same intimate simplicity of phrase. Death, and the death of one so dear, is no matter for rhetoric. And even for Cleopatra, attired in all her splendor, Charmian finds the simplest of terms: "a lass unparalleled." And Macbeth, when the news of his wife's death is brought him, can find no words whatever. How far we are in all these from Romeo's grief, and almost as far from Horatio's "flights of angels."

[60] From now until the beginning of Othello's last speech Lodovico should dominate the scene. Actors of Othello are too apt to believe that, even from "It is the cause, it is the cause, my soul. . . ," to the end, the responsibility rests upon them. But Shakespeare has been careful to relieve them from such a strain, and the scene itself from the monotony involved. Emilia's masterful intervention, Iago's attack on her, his flight and her death provide such relief. And now, for a while, Othello remains an all but passive figure, and, for a little, before his

> Soft you; a word or two before you go. . . .

is an all but silent one. By which passivity the dramatic value of his last speech, when he does make it, is notably increased.

—should answer the question one way or the other. But at Lodovico's peremptory

Wrench his sword from him.

he is for the second time disarmed; and Iago, though he wince, can vaunt diabolically enough:

I bleed, sir, but not killed.

The tension is relaxed by Othello's rueful, sardonic:

I am not sorry neither: I'ld have thee live;
For, in my sense, 'tis happiness to die.

This kindles the compassionate reproach of Lodovico's

O, thou, Othello, that wert once so good,
Fallen in the practice of a damned slave,
What shall be said to thee?

which finds answer in the terse

Why, any thing;
An honourable murderer, if you will;
For nought I did in hate but all in honour.

An honorable murderer! Is there more to be said?

Lodovico continues his inquest. Each there has his part in it, and by an individual touch or two helps to sustain and diversify the fabric of the scene. The wounded Cassio's response to Othello's single-syllabled, abased avowal of intent to murder him, is but a grieved

Dear general, I never gave you cause.

As unaffected a

I do believe it, and I ask your pardon.

recalls—if nothing could restore—the old frank comradeship between the two.

And what more cause had this other?

Will you, I pray, demand that demi-devil
Why he hath thus ensnared my soul and body?

Does Iago even know the answer? "I hate the Moor," rabidly, senselessly, profitlessly; a search through the ruin of his tricks and lies would add nothing real to that. And in the light of the consequences—for him also—such an answer must seem almost less tragic than absurd. Incorrigibly he wraps himself in the shreds of his satanic conceit, as self-deceived in this, it may be, as were his victims in their "honest" Iago:

> Demand me nothing; what you know, you know.
> From this time forth I never will speak word.

And if the ordeal will be sharp, the hardihood of vanity is great. Lodovico's shocked

> What, not to pray?

Gratiano's exasperated

> Torments will ope your lips.

are, at each extreme, the habitual human response to such contumacy. Othello's indifferent

> Well, thou dost best.

speaks of weary readiness to have done with it all.

But he must be held to life's business still; so the magistral Lodovico, showing him some respect, insists:

> Sir, you shall understand what hath befallen,
> Which, as I think, you know not. . . .

The last is heard of the paltry handkerchief. He confirms Emilia's judgment:

> O, fool! fool! fool!

Then the rest turn, as men will with grave matters concluded, to talk more volubly of the lesser. Here it is of the

> letter
> Found in the pocket of the slain Roderigo . . .

and of "another discontented paper," and of the trick played on Cassio which led to his disgrace, and of Roderigo's wonderful recovery. And how much more of the sort would there not be to say, but that Lodovico once more gives orders.[61]

[61] This diverting of our attention at such a moment from Othello to the papers found in Roderigo's pocket has been a matter of distress to certain commentators. Koester, in particular, to quote from the Furness Variorum, finding here "in the needlessness of these letters, and in the fact that they rehearse only what is

Othello must to prison. As they prepare to conduct him there he speaks:

Soft you; a word or two before you go. . . .

The old quiet authority is his again in fullest measure; a touch of irony added here. Before *they* go. Give orders now who may, he will not. Then:

I have done the state some service and they know it. . . .

—his one dispassionate comment upon his downfall from what he was. For the rest, let them speak the truth of him, and of those "unlucky deeds"; and the mild detachment of the phrase tells them that he himself knows it, as a man may when nothing is left him of either hope or fear. They are to speak

Of one that loved not wisely but too well;
Of one not easily jealous, but, being wrought,
Perplexed in the extreme . . .

It is the truth.

of one whose hand,
Like the base Indian, threw a pearl away
Richer than all his tribe; of one whose subdued eyes,
Albeit unused to the melting mood,
Drop tears as fast as the Arabian trees
Their medicinal gum. . . .

---

already known to the audience, a proof that the scenes, in which the events related in these letters occur, were omitted in the representation."

But it is, of course, only another example—of which the play holds several—of preparing for a passage of supreme tension, such as Othello's last speech will be, by one in which the tension is slack. That Shakespeare did not think of the letters and of Roderigo's recovery until he suddenly found he had need of something of the sort—of this there are signs. Was the letter that "imports the death of Cassio" written by Iago? When?—not to mention why? And was he, the tried soldier, such a bungler with sword and dagger that he could not competently dispatch the already wounded Roderigo?

But these are idle arguments. The dramatic purpose of the passage is plain enough: to take our attention temporarily from Othello, so that when he recaptures it he will do so the more impressively. Material for such a passage must not be of first importance, or the tension will not be slackened; nor, at such a critical moment, can it be of merely extraneous interest, or our attention will be dissipated. The Roderigo-Iago-Cassio complication, with a final reference to the handkerchief, seems, then, to fill the need and suit the occasion fairly well. And far from the inconsistencies involved and the pedestrian style being evidence that Shakespeare did not write the passage, admit its dramatic utility, and they could perhaps better be pleaded as evidence that he did.

No longer cruel tears; and the crude horror of the deed done already tempered a little—Nature's healing sadness would be at work. But not in him. He knows better than they can tell him or Venice decide what is due to an Othello, traitor to his Christian self, from him who is now that self again; and this they shall see. Therefore,

> say besides, that in Aleppo once,
> Where a malignant and a turbaned Turk
> Beat a Venetian, and traduced the state,
> I took by the throat the circumcised dog,
> And smote him, thus.

—twice they have disarmed him, but he had kept a dagger hidden.

Gratiano and Lodovico cry out at the sight. Cassio does not; his comment comes later:

> This did I fear, but thought he had no weapon;
> For he was great of heart.

—homage to his lost hero overriding prescribed disapproval. Othello, the while, lies dead, with the dead Desdemona in his arms:

> I kissed thee ere I killed thee; no way but this,
> Killing myself, to die upon a kiss.

The simple rhyme and the simple sentiment harbor peace in oblivion.

But Lodovico turns our eyes once more upon Iago:

> O, Spartan dog,
> More fell than anguish, hunger, or the sea.
> Look on the tragic loading of this bed;
> This is thy work. . . .

In Iago's stressed silence, as he looks, is the last stroke of the action. His face is an inscrutable mask. What lies behind that but the stupidity of evil?

Act and Scene Division

Q1 and F1, near of a date in their printing, which was some eighteen to twenty years subsequent to the play's writing and staging, agree—but for a slip or so, fairly patent as such—upon its act and scene division.

The scene-division is in any case indicated in the action itself by the "cleared stage."[62] Localization, except for the first three scenes and the last, is less than precise. But the action demands this.[63]

As to the act-division; this has (exceptionally) sufficient purely dramatic validity, is sufficiently a part of the play's articulation, for it to be at least claimable—despite the twenty-year lag—as Shakespeare's own. Act I is indubitably a unit of action. Act II may be accounted one also, if not so completely, since Iago's "By the mass, 'tis morning. . . ." and Cassio's later "The day had broke before we parted. . . ." link II and III closely together. Act V has unity of subject. It compasses all the murderous consequences of Iago's scheming, and in it the whole action is wound up. There seems only to be no good reason why Acts III and IV should be divided as they are—or indeed at all—unless it be to make up the classic count of five. If this should be the purpose, the division is doubtless as good a one as may be. It shares the total matter of the two acts approximately in halves, and the flow of the action can be said to move more swiftly and fatally towards catastrophe—and markedly so—in Act IV than in Act III.

But act-division may be made to mean, in the actual staging of a play, more than one thing; a short formal pause of relaxation, or a prolonged interval in which the audience can move about and the sympathetic contact established with the actors will be broken, or anything between the two; and the effect upon the performance will be very different. What the practice of the theater was, either at the time of the play's writing or of its printing twenty years later, we do not know. Five acts smacks somewhat of the respectability of editing and printing, and F1 has certainly imposed the formula upon some plays that Shakespeare himself never so shaped. But it does not follow that he never so shaped any. *Henry V* at least, in fact, he did. Nor does it follow that three acts or four may not have suited him as well if that suited his subject. He and his theater were not bound to the classic rule for its own sake, and it can have meant little to his audience. Why indeed—so free was he—should he plan his

[62] The trivial complication concerning the Herald is noted in its place.

[63] Cf. p. 51, note 27; p. 65, note 40.

plays to any so unyielding a measure as "acts" at all? To some significant pattern, inevitably, his play must be shaped. If this allowed for a relaxing pause or so convenient to actors and audience and of benefit to its performance, so much the better. And if in time the five acts became an established formula for the theater as for the printed page, and four interrupting intervals in a performance promised to be too many, the superfluous ones had only to be formalized, even to vanishing point—Shakespeare and his immediate inheritors were masters enough in a theater of their own making for that; and that, I suggest, is how they would view the matter.

The producer of Shakespeare's plays today, in this as in more important questions, must distinguish the essential from the incidental. Where direct evidence is lacking as authority for what he aims to do he must fall back on circumstantial, judging the worth of it. He must, on occasions, boldly deduce the particular from the general; this being his own general knowledge of the essentials of Shakespeare's art, his title to produce the plays at all. He need not claim to be impeccably correct in what he does. He cannot wait for positive proof over this or that disputed point; he must do something. In the small matter of this play's act-division his course is, however, both easy and pretty plain. He should not, very certainly, introduce act-divisions of his own devising; nor does he need to, with four already provided, which are on the whole more likely to be Shakespeare's than not. He need not, on the other hand, give the value of a prolonged interval to what may have in Shakespeare's own theater counted merely as a formal pause. Nor if—the evidence being what it is—he overrides an act-division altogether (say, that in particular between Acts III and IV) will he commit any deadly sin; for he can plead that he is but emphasizing the general continuity of action, which is one of the "essentials in ordinary" of Shakespeare's art.

The Characters

IAGO

If Iago presents something of a problem to the critic, so did he to Shakespeare. It was not a question first of imagining the man and then of finding the appropriate thing for him to do. What was to happen had already in the main been settled—by Cinthio; Shakespeare's task was to devise a character who could take his allotted share in this, convincingly and effectively.

Cinthio is in no difficulty. He warrants his "wicked Ensign" capable of every necessary crime simply by describing him as "a man of the most depraved nature in the world," and thereafter telling us that this or the other happened in the tone of one who—the events being over and done with—fears no contradiction. But the dramatist is by no means so taken at his word. His characters, under our scrutiny, must convince us of the likelihood of what they do even as they do it, while every word they speak is compulsory evidence of what they are. Carried through on such terms, the Ensign's task in the story—Iago's in the play, and Shakespeare's—can be no easy one.

Out of Cinthio's Moor Shakespeare molds to his own liking the heroic Othello, confident, dignified, candid, calm. He sets up an Iago in total contrast to him; a common fellow, foul-minded and coarse-tongued, a braggart decrying in others the qualities he himself lacks, bitterly envious, pettily spiteful, morbidly vain. He has abounding vitality, a glib tongue and a remarkable faculty of adapting himself to his company, as we see when the cynical swagger which so impresses Roderigo—that portentous "I am not what I am" and the like—turns to sober soldierly modesty with Othello. Since Iago in the course of the play will attitudinize much and variously, and not only before his victims but to himself, will exhibit such skill and a seemingly all but supernatural cunning, Shakespeare, for a start, gives us this unvarnished view of him, of the self, at any rate, that he shows to Roderigo, whom he despises too much to care to cheat of anything but money.

We could take it, too, that this opening view of Iago, the first impression he is to make, was meant to be the true one, if only because Shakespeare, in first presenting a character, never deliberately misleads us, is accustomed, rather, to sketch in its chief features, then and there, as unmistakably as possible, so as to leave us in no doubt from the start as to the sort of man or woman he is.[64] He likes, moreover, to state his case—so to say—as soon and as clearly as possible. And here, in the first two scenes, in the contrast between the men, and in the boasted hate and its masking, are the main factors of the play already defined and set in motion. We shall, besides, soon become aware that a play is in the making differing in important aspects from its neighbor tragedies. With Macbeth, with Antony, amid the clashes of *King Lear*, the destructive force is one of the nobler human ardors turned to evil, and the battleground—as so notably with Hamlet—is the hero's soul. Here the evil impulse is externalized in Iago; and if Othello's soul be a battleground, he himself puts up no fight on it. Nor can the jealousy which undoes him be properly called a degrading of the love it supplants; it is an aberration rather, and an ignoble one. Iago inoculates him with it, as with a disease, and after the feeblest of struggles against it—he is lost.[65] Othello is not, therefore, a spiritual tragedy in the sense that the others may be called so. It is only the more painful; an all but intolerable exhibition, indeed, of human wickedness and folly, which does not so much purge us with pity and terror as fill us with horror and with anger that such a shoddy creature as Iago, possessed by his mountebank egoism, his envy and spite, should be able unresisted to destroy an Othello and bring Desdemona to her death. This incongruity is the keynote of the tragedy, and Shakespeare, therefore, strikes it clearly to begin with. And the actor who tries, here or later, to present Iago as a sort of half-brother to Milton's Satan only falsifies both character and play.

To begin with he is not planning Othello's ruin at all. While he protests that

> I do hate him as I do hell pains. . . .

yet for an aim:

> I follow him to serve my turn upon him. . . .

[64] I can think of no instance to the contrary. It will be partly, of course, a question of economy. He has much to do with his characters—their talk and action make up his sole medium—and not overmuch time in which to do it. He cannot afford to turn them first in one direction, then in another, and so complicate his task.

[65] Cf. Leontes, whom Shakespeare, writing later, treats as a purely pathological case.

and he admits that Brabantio's anger can at most only

gall him to some check . . .

Roderigo do no more than

poison his delight , . .
And though he in a fertile climate dwell,
Plague him with flies. . . .

Spite; nothing deadlier! And when later, left alone, he asks himself how he may best serve his turn upon him, it will be by filching Cassio's place; and simply to this end it is that he intends

After some time, to abuse Othello's ear
That he is too familiar with his wife.

It will no doubt gratify his malice merely to see Othello vexed by jealousy (that being, it seems, the one sort of barb by which his own hide might be pierced); and a finer-drawn second thought ensues, another vista is opened in the

and to plume up my will
In double knavery . . .

—to flatter and foster, besides, that is to say, his egregious conceit of his own wickedness.[66] But he is still aiming in the main at his own material advantage. Well for him, it will seem in retrospect, had he looked no further and known when to "cash in" on a success. For within a while, by his plausible tongue and his gangster's skill, he will most brilliantly have maneuvered Cassio

[66] Bradley, after much debate, finds in the "plume up my will . . ." the master-key to Iago's mind, his inmost motive. To agree one must add, I think, that Iago is hardly aware of it—nor Shakespeare. This is not necessarily the paradox it may sound. An imaginative author, steeped in his subject, will sometimes write more wisely than he knows. One need only insist, then, that Shakespeare is not here intentionally presenting us with any such master-key; for if he were he would give the phrase an appropriate saliency, whereas it is so placed in the speech that it cannot well be made either arresting or memorable. In the "double knavery" does come the first hint of the will to do evil for its own sake (as well as for the profit of it) that carries Iago both to triumph and disaster, but one cannot recognize the tune from this single note heard in passing.

Bradley was a most enlightened critic and one hesitates to differ from him. But his habit of treating the characters in a play as if they had once lived actual lives of their own (he says elsewhere, for instance, that Iago's intellect cannot be compared to Napoleon's; but one must not, surely, even begin to compare an imaginary Iago to a real Napoleon), while it lends his pages great vitality, is apt to blind him to mere dramatic technicalities such as this.

into disgrace, and still be "honest Iago" to all the world, his victim included. And there is the lieutenantry ripe and ready to fall to him. But by then he must be appeasing the hunger of his quite profitless hate for Othello. Here are deeper waters. Success exhilarating him, he plunges in, to find that seemingly he can navigate them as brilliantly. He wins his will, and no hate could be more fully satisfied. But it is at the price of his own torture and death; no part of the program, this! There is this tragedy of Iago to be considered too, though it will hardly appeal to our pity.

What is the secret of his success—and failure? If it rests, as is likely, in his being what he is, he cannot tell us, and we listen to those many soliloquies in vain. Of his opinions and desires and of what he means to do they will tell us truly; but as to what he *is*, less than another can the man who lives by deceiving others know the truth about himself. We observe and must judge for ourselves. He vaunts his doctrine of "reason," and seemingly wiser ears than Roderigo's have approved that

> 'tis in ourselves that we are thus or thus. . . . If the balance of our lives had not the one scale of reason to poise another of sensuality, the blood and baseness of our natures would conduct us to most preposterous conclusions. . . .

—as, in fact, the blood and baseness of Iago's nature ultimately do. He owes it, then, to his intellectual vanity to make a show of finding good reason for wreaking his hate on Othello. But it is a very poor show. He cannot trouble even to decide whether he thinks that Othello has cuckolded him or no.

> I know not if't be true,
> But I, for mere suspicion in that kind,
> Will do as if for surety.

Suspicion of "the lusty Moor" (about the last epithet, incidentally, to apply to Othello) is, however, of itself so encouraging, that he returns to it, yet to admit besides in the very next breath that

> The Moor, howbeit that I endure him not,
> Is of a constant, loving, noble nature;
> And I dare think he'll prove to Desdemona
> A most dear husband. . . .

—to which incongruous testimony he tags a fantastic notion of fastening upon Desdemona himself; since

> I do love her too,
> Not out of absolute lust . . .
> But partly led to diet my revenge. . . .

next contributing to this mental chaos a sudden parenthetic

> For I fear Cassio with my night-cap too . . .

(the recent, frank, merrily gallant kiss of greeting offered Emilia twisted to that account!). Needless to say we hear no more of his "love" for Desdemona or fear of Cassio. And his suspicion of Othello's lechery, stoked up to

> the thought whereof
> Doth like a poisonous mineral gnaw my inwards;
> And nothing can or shall content my soul
> Till I am evened with him, wife for wife. . . .

collapses, inconsequently and ridiculously, then and there, into

> Or failing so, yet that I put the Moor
> At least into a jealousy so strong
> That judgment cannot cure. . . .

By the light of his reasoning, then—this being a specimen of it —Iago would not seem likely to get very far. Nor is his judgment of Othello's character oversound. Nor, when he turns to Desdemona—with

> That Cassio loves her, I do well believe it;
> That she loves him, 'tis apt and of great credit. . . .

—does he come nearer the mark; and even as to Cassio he is astray. And the soliloquy's ending, its

> 'Tis here, but yet confused. . . .

suggests that he is not wholly unaware of all this himself. It is not "reason" that serves him, though he would like to think it did. We note, too, that his projects are continually changing. It is on the spur of the moment that he is at his best, when he trusts to its inspiration.

Swinburne, refining upon Hazlitt, calls Iago "a contriving artist in real life," and the phrase is illuminating. Here indeed is the key—and was there need of any other?—to the problem

Shakespeare set himself when he decided that his heroic Othello was not to be destroyed by an opponent of the same caliber, but dragged down by an Iago. He will not, that is to say, exalt such wickedness. That Iago himself should do so—the clever, but essentially stupid fellow, the common man of common mind—is quite another matter. But how equip such a one for his task, with genuine capacities denied him? By endowing him with the intuition of the artist, and the power of counterfeiting them. And Shakespeare will have a further need, which an artist Iago can satisfy, of a villain pursuing wickedness for its own sake.

The artist in leading-strings, writing or painting or making music to order, may be a happily harmless creature enough. Love of his art for its own sake turns him egoist. This is inevitable. In normal human love for a person, a country or a cause, we find egoism and devotion combined, the egoism storing up no more force than will be spent in devotion. But the artist's devotion to his evolving work is to something that is still a part of him, and his egoism will thus be fed and fed until the completing of the work discharges him of its burden. Being ill-fed or over-fed, it may grow diseased and monstrous. The force of a passion so self-fulfilling as to be self-forgetful is likeliest, perhaps, to carry him cleanly through the adventure; and this, at its most powerful, can so mobilize his faculties that their functions will seem to fuse—imagination and thought and skill working together as one—to an incommunicable magnifying of their power. The artist-egoist, minding nothing but his art, can, of course, be as harmless a creature—unless to himself and his friends and relations—as the artist in leading-strings, and his work may have its peculiar value. But set such an occult and lawless force operating in real life, and it can prove dangerous indeed; this force in Iago, for instance, of a love of evil for its own sake, vivified by the artist's powers, pursued with the artist's unscrupulous passion.

The medium in which Iago works is the actor's; and in the crude sense of pretending to be what he is not, and in his chameleonlike ability to adapt himself to change of company and circumstance, we find him an accomplished actor from the beginning. These rudiments of the art of acting most people learn to practice a little—and harmlessly—in real life; but Iago is an expert to the point that pretense is second nature to him. In his earlier maneuverings, moreover, he is on familiar ground. "Honest Iago," with his sympathetically parasitic faculty of being all things to all men, knows, without thinking, how his fellow soldiers Cassio and Montano (Roderigo is a nonentity), the Cyprus gallants and Othello will think and act when events pass—with a very little help from him—as they do. So all goes well. Then, under their stimulus of success, and triflingly perhaps of wine,[67] his inherent hatred of Othello begins to pulse more urgently, and then it is that the artist in Iago takes effective command. For his profit in Cassio's ruin, already achieved, is forgotten, and it is the thought of Othello's that obsesses him, profitless though this may be. Here is the artist who will do the thing for its own sake, and out of sheer delight in the doing let himself be carried beyond all bounds of "reason" and prudence. Desdemona shall be ruined too, though he has no hatred for her. And, beaconlike, there at once flashes on him—as inspiration visits the artist—a solution to the problem that his reason left so confused. An error to speculate, as his own nature bade him, upon Cassio's treachery to his friend, Desdemona's to Othello. It is the very virtues of the virtuous that can best be turned against them. While Cassio, therefore,

> this honest fool
> Plies Desdemona to repair his fortunes,
> And she for him pleads strongly to the Moor,
> I'll pour this pestilence into his ear,
> That she repeals him for her body's lust;
> And by how much she strives to do him good,
> She shall undo her credit with the Moor.
> So will I turn her virtue into pitch;
> And out of her own goodnesss make the net
> That shall enmesh them all.

Iago feels—as at such a moment the fervent artist will—that a very revelation has been vouchsafed him, sent direct from the Devil himself, so exhilarating is it. And Shakespeare has found, in part at least, the Iago he needs. And the way is now open to the play's tragic end.

[67] That which hath made Cassio drunk hath made him bold. Lady Macbeth had the same head for liquor.

But given the unqualified purpose, what of the task itself and the means? To undermine Othello's faith in Desdemona! What part can Iago play which will best let him attempt that? Of the hectoring admonition which serves with Roderigo there can naturally be none, nor much, to begin with at any rate, of the frank comradely helpfulness which is bait for Cassio. Can any sort of frontal attack, indeed, be made on that superb authority? Somehow, then, he must find his way behind the defenses, and from there, in the friendliest fashion, help Othello to achieve his own ruin. Hate, moreover, dictates this, since there is no ill worse than self-inflicted ill. But how insinuate his way into that very sanctuary of Othello's being where love for Desdemona is lodged? How discover in his own base nature enough understanding of Othello's to admit him there? How qualify for the playing of this part?

Play-acting is pretense, and as an art it is more than that. The actor is the dramatist's mouthpiece, and as an artist he is something besides. His share in their mutual work is to give bodily life to what has until then existed only as thought recorded in words. The career of a character in a play from its imagining to its presenting on a stage has something in common with the begetting and birth of a child, and the particular shares of the parents in their offspring may both seem as obvious and prove as hard to analyze. But an actor will acquire certain specialized and somewhat anomalous faculties. Being neither mere mouthpiece nor mere puppet, he interprets a character—the material the dramatist gives him—in the terms, more or less disguised, of his own personality. Yet it will not be his true personality. He cannot, strictly speaking, know more of the character than the dramatist has told him, and this, though it be the essential part, can never be much. But he must seem to know much more, and in many ways, if we are to think of the two as one. Yet this need be but seeming. He need acquire no knowledge but apparent knowledge, cultivate in this respect no ability but to seem able, nor build up, of this composite personality demanded, anything but a painted façade. Note that it is not a question of trivial knowledge or poor ability, still less of evil or good, but of knowledge and ability merely reflected as in a mirror—which reflects the best and the worthless alike. The actor's is, above all, the faculty of sympathy; found physically in the sensitive ear, the receptive eye, the dancer's body that of itself responds, emotionally in the tears or laughter ready at call, and intellectually in a capacity not only seemingly to absorb some product of another's thought, but to reproduce the effects of understanding it without necessarily having understood it in the least. The mirror upheld to nature is a long-accepted image for the art of the theater. As the art matures the mirror is brought to reflecting from beneath the surface; and in the character and skill of an Iago is pictured to us—a reflection from art back to life again—how bedded in human nature and active in real life the actor's faculty can be. In real life also it *may* be innocuously exercised; the worst to be urged as a rule against the parasite intelligence—to which dishonorable status the loss of artistic sanction reduces the actor's—a certain complacency in futility. But with hate to give it purpose, it can be made, as Iago makes it, an instrument of deadly corruption.

He has most sensitive material to work upon. Othello—it is the countervailing trait to his soldierly calm—is as quick in response to a touch or a hint as the high-mettled barb he would ride. And if Iago wisely cannot, neither has he need to accuse Desdemona directly and brutally. A little eavesdropping gives him for a starting point matter which is in Othello's mind already, a known answer to his artless question whether Cassio knew of the wooing. From there he feels his way—as delicately at first as an insect by its tentacles—into that field of the man's affections in which he means to make havoc; and he surreptitiously takes and ever so slightly twists the form of the matter he finds there and reflects it back to Othello, who sees his own thought again as in a distorting mirror, receives back thoughts and words obscured and perverted. He cannot dominate Othello yet, but he can misinterpret him to himself.

The finer the nature the more fragile its defense; when thicker skins would be but chafed, the poison permeates Othello. For a measure of his susceptibility: it needs but the provocative intonation of that single word "Indeed" to set him questioning, and again questioning, insistent to be answered, and to leave him to self-questioning. Here is the intuitively feared requital for the "content so absolute" of his reunion with Desdemona; no halfway for him between that and a very helplessness of doubt. And Iago, admitted to intimacy, can not only proffer, for bad example, his own failings in jealousy and suspicion, but—his parasite mind feeding on Othello's, his coarse spirit gaining perception from contact with Othello's fine spirit—can soon learn to detect rifts in the texture of its confidence made ready for his widening that Othello will then himself the more effectively widen again. "By heaven," he exclaims, "he echoes me"; and words and thoughts are indeed flung back and forth between them until it would be hard to say whose they first were. And note how Iago seizes on the vague misgiving in the unfinished thought of Desdemona's nature "erring from itself—" to shape and color it into a vivid image of her, rank of "will" and foul of mind; it is such a verdict on her very love for him that he renders back to Othello, to be digested and turned about, and to re-emerge, its stigma on them both, in the bitter "Haply, for I am black. . . ."

In this passage of less than two hundred lines we are shown Othello's moral disintegration. But it owes its compressed form and continuity to dramatic convenience only. Actually to be imagined is a protracted, many-sided, disjunctive process of chicanery, in which Iago gathers, mainly from Othello himself, how best to cheat him, a complexity which Shakespeare clarifies and orders into the form of a few minutes' talk, into no greater a space than the action allowable can animate.

Iago is enjoying himself. He has the artist's faculty for doing well whatever he takes pleasure in doing, and for no solider reason than that. He is even amusing himself. The trick with the handkerchief—"This may do something"—should prove a pretty one. He has yet to see the effect of his poison on Othello. It will doubtless soon begin to "Burn like the mines of sulphur," but he can hardly look suddenly to find his obliging self in the clutch of that "waked wrath," and being shaken as a rat by a dog.

He is a passionless creature. Cinthio gives his wicked Ensign some motive for evil-doing in jealousy, and a love for Desdemona ignored and so "changed into the bitterest hate." But Shakespeare admits neither love nor lust into Iago's composition, nothing so human; shows him to us, on the contrary, frigidly speculating upon the use such indulgence might be to him, and as frigidly deciding: none. Even his hate is cold, and will be the more tenacious for that, its strength not being spent in emotional ebb and flow. His endeavors then to respond suitably to Othello's outbursts—the flamboyant "Take note, take note, O world . . ." and the kneeling to echo and to mock the oath by "yond marble heaven"—are simply histrionic, and overdone at that. And this, made plain to us, might be plain to Othello, were he not "eaten up with passion." For of intellectual excitement Iago *is* capable, and, elated by swift success, he begins to run risks. That stirs his cold blood; it is all that does. And the pleasures of the game, as it develops, are multiplying. He has the noble Moor stripped now, but for a rag or so, of his nobility; no stimulus to savagery seems to be too strong for him. Iago can, consequently, admit more of himself into the part he is playing, can, in the actor's phrase, "let himself go," while the actor faculty enables him still to keep a cool enough eye upon whither he is going. He can thus vent the full foulness of his mind, in itself a relief and a pleasure: and there is the sheer pleasure of seeing Othello suffer and madden beneath the spate of it. And his daring pays. The success of the enterprise betters all expectation. Not merely is Cassio's death to be granted him—and he had schemed for no more than his disgrace—but at that zestful crisis, with the artist in evil in him strung to perfect pitch, one timely phrase assures him of Desdemona's thrown in too.

But in the very ease and abundance of his success, in his complacent enjoyment and exploitation of it, looking neither ahead nor around, lie the means to his ultimate ruin. To harry the distraught Othello until he actually collapses at his feet in a fit, then to rally the unlucky cuckold and condescendingly urge him to "be a man"; to be able to jerk him, like a black puppet, back and forth from his eavesdropping—what could be more amusing? And having once had to defer for his ends to each changing shade of Othello's mood, now to find the victim swaying to every sinister touch, even to be able—artist in evil as he is—to devise that felicitous strangling of Desdemona "in her bed, even the bed she hath contaminated"—this is gratifying too. There are secret satisfactions besides. To see Desdemona struck and be the hidden force behind the blow, to deplore Othello's conduct and be the unsuspected prompter of it; this is meat and drink to thwarted, perverted vanity. And that the blind fools who have ever galled him by their patronizing praise should be deaf to the irony in his

> Alas, alas!
> It is not *honesty* in me to speak
> What I have seen and known.

—he finds egregious pleasure here.

Then comes, as an unlooked-for gift, the most delectable episode in his clandestine triumph. He has seen Othello collapsed at his feet; now it is Desdemona kneeling there, innocently begging the humble Ensign to rescue her from the very misery—did she but know it, worse!—into which he, even he, has plunged her. He savors her anguish, gently encourages the pitiful delusion. Could his tortuous "Divinity of hell" be more gracious to him—yet, fittingly, and as invariably under surfeit of good luck, more beguiling? For in the cold, complacent arrogance of his success he disregards and dismisses with a dozen contemptuous words, with a final "You are a fool: go to," the threat that, at this very moment, emerges so plainly and sounds so insistently in Emilia's questing anger. Here again shows the radical stupidity of the man, that other aspect of the adroit, intuitively extemporizing artist-actor-charlatan, who until now has played his deadly part so well. He misjudges Emilia, even as by the light of his vaunted "reason" he misjudged Desdemona and Cassio as likely lovers and traitors to Othello. He may know the Emilia of a marriage to him. How should such as he divine what fellowship with Desdemona has made her?

This complacency adds even to the careless contempt with which he customarily treats Roderigo, now unexpectedly rebellious. When he sees that the trouble is serious he schemes its liquidation—and Roderigo's—smartly enough; and Cassio's death in addition will round off events very comfortably. But his luck proves to be a little out, that "devil's own luck" which has carried him round so many awkward corners—which is perhaps but another term for the quick sense of the effective moment that has marked him at his best. Roderigo blunders. He blunders. It is not irretrievable blundering, but it rattles him. And he, whose cue it is to be always so cool and detached, finds himself bustling, too, amid the bustle and confusion, and bluffing and giving orders at random. And for the very first time—although not until he has said it does he really recognize it:

> This is the night
> That either makes me, or fordoes me quite.

—he is touched by fear.

When Emilia turns on him and speaks out and stands her ground he is utterly at a loss, can find nothing to do but stupidly, since uselessly, to kill her.

In the Folio's list of characters Iago is ticketed "a Villaine," as he might be in the program of the crudest of melodramas today; and he himself rejoices in his claims to the title. Even so, and yet more explicitly, does Richard III announce in his first soliloquy that he is "determined to prove a villain," proceed accordingly, and, in his last, argue at some length the metaphysical issues of his conduct. But between the writing of the two plays Shakespeare has developed other methods. He has learned to take these theatrical types and to give them, not merely more individuality, but an inward verity as well. Out of the conventional Jew comes Shylock; Falstaff out of Prince Hal's butt and buffoon; out of the "melancholy man" Hamlet. And out of Cinthio's "wicked Ensign," and his theatrical match, the melodramatic "villaine," evolves Iago.

Points of view will remain, from which a line drawn between Iago and the villain of melodrama is so fine as to be invisible. But melodrama is not necessarily false to life; it may only unduly simplify it. And Shakespeare's problem was to retain the melodramatic simplicity with the strength which belongs to it, and to give this an inward verity too. He solves it, as we have seen, by making his Iago something of a melodramatic actor in real life. The result is a highly complex, and at moments a very puzzling, character; but in it the reconciliation between verity and melodrama is achieved. There are plenty such people in the world, who borrow, as actors do, their working material, may add bits of themselves to it, will make a superficially brilliant use of the amalgam, yet remain worthless within. But, as a rule, they lack force of character (again, as do actors, they "live to please"), and the Iago of the story must be exceptionally endowed with some sort of force. Shakespeare sees this begotten by hate, and by a hate which will have only the more force for being unreasoning and motiveless.[68] In its stupidity—there is to be no glorification of such wickedness—it can well bring him at last to his doom, but by a blinkered persistence which belongs to unreason it may first attain its ends. Iago—it belongs to the part he is playing—sees himself above all as a man of reason. He reminds us rather, behind his intellectual antics, of a hound on the trail, sensitive and alert, nose to the mud, searching and sampling, appetite and instinct combining to guide him past error after error to his quarry. His hate possesses him. It rewards him. But when it has had its will of him he is left—a swaggering mountebank still. The broken, bewildered Othello asks:

> Will you, I pray, demand that demi-devil
> Why he hath thus ensnared my soul and body?

Why, indeed! The true answer, spuriously qualified, he has long ago given us—and Roderigo. Repeated amid this holocaust, would it not sound even to him so incongruous as to be all but comic? "I hate the Moor"—there has been no more to the whole elaborately wicked business than that.

But with passion and persistence and some plausibility and the narrowness of purpose that belongs to evil, what cannot stupidity achieve?

OTHELLO

We have seen how, to make the story dramatically viable, the mainspring of the play's action has to be drastically compressed. It follows that the fatal flaw in the hero's character must be one which will develop swiftly and catastrophically too. The story has provided in sexual jealousy about the only one which will.

Of vanity, envy, self-seeking and distrust, which are the seeds of jealousy in general, Othello, it is insisted from the beginning, is notably free, so free that he will not readily remark them in others—in Iago, for instance, in whom they so richly abound.

[68] Cinthio gives his "wicked Ensign" a motive in a one-time love for Desdemona, which, ignored, has "changed into the bitterest hate." But Shakespeare—instead of seizing on it as a human contribution to his villainy—rejects this.

And he has never yet cared enough for a woman to be jealous of her; that also is made clear. It is a nature, then, taught by no earlier minor failings of this kind to resist a gross attack on it, should that come.

But sexual jealousy, once given rein, is a passion like no other. It is pathological, a moral lesion, a monomania. Facts and reason become its playthings. Othello does at first put up a feeble intellectual resistance, in a single soliloquy he struggles a little with himself; but, after this, every defense is swept away, and the poison rages in him unchecked. Here, then, is the sudden and swift descent to catastrophe, which the story, as Shakespeare dramatizes it, demands. A bad business, certainly, yet, to this extent, shocking rather than tragic. Indeed, did not Othello suffer so and dispense suffering, the spectacle of his wholly baseless duping and befooling would be more comic than otherwise, a mere upsetting of his confidence and dignity, as enjoyable to us as to Iago; and, in a ghastly fashion, it for a few moments becomes so when he is set eavesdropping upon Cassio and Bianca. Shocking, that it is, and pitiful, for all perplexed suffering is pitiful. But there is more to true tragedy than this.

The writing and rewriting of *Hamlet* must surely have shown Shakespeare the limits to the dramatic use that can be made of the purely pathological. For while little was to be done in exhibiting the character of a man consistently aping madness who would not reveal himself, even less was practicable if he were really mad and could not. With Hamlet it is the land near the borderline which proves peculiarly fruitful, since there we have him so acutely conscious of himself as to be at his readiest for that work of self-purgation by which the tragic hero finds significance in his fate.

With Othello neither the planning of the play, nor his character, nor the jealous mania which is foreign to every other trait in it, will allow for this. He cannot reason with himself about something which is in its very nature unreasonable, nor can Shakespeare set him searching for the significance of events which exist only in Iago's lies—we, the audience, should resent such futility. He is betrayed and goes ignorantly to his doom.

And when, at last, Desdemona dead, he learns the truth, what can he have to say—or we!—but

O, fool, fool, fool!

The mere sight of such beauty and nobility and happiness, all wickedly destroyed, must be a harrowing one. Yet the pity and terror of it come short of serving for the purgation of our souls, since Othello's own soul stays unpurged. Hamlet dies spiritually at peace; Lear's madness has been the means to his salvation; by interpreting his life's hell to us even Macbeth stirs us to some compassion. But what alchemy can now bring the noble Moor and the savage murderer into unity again? The "cruel tears" and the kiss and the talk of justice are more intolerable than the savagery itself. Nor can remorse bridge—though too late—the gulf between the two; they were and remain beings apart. Othello wakes as from a nightmare only to kill himself, his prospect hell. And the play's last word is, significantly, not of him, but of tortures for Iago; punishment as barren as the crime. It is a tragedy without meaning, and that is the ultimate horror of it.

But Othello, when it is too late, does at least become conscious of this cleavage made in his nature. Hence his submission to Lodovico as

he that *was* Othello . . .

The Othello that was could never have done such a deed; an ignorant brute in him has done it. Yet it is still he, the Christian Othello, accepted, trusted, loved, who has proved viler even than "the circumcised dog" that he smote "in Aleppo once." It is the fellow to this dog in him that he now smites "thus" to end all.

If he cannot be let elucidate his calamities, Shakespeare can at least make him the very kind of man who could not. To begin with, he is "the Moor," and in this alone, a strange, removed, enigmatic figure. Before we see him we hear him only vilified as "thick-lips" and "lascivious Moor"; it is a way of adding by slight surprise to the effect he will make upon us when he does appear, so plainly nothing of the sort, but—even before we learn he is of royal blood—an aristocrat, a chief of men and the ripe soldier, sparing of words, their tone level and clear, not to be flustered or overawed. He will have no street-brawling; that is not how he fights when he must fight. Nor will he wrangle here in public;

he does not even notice Brabantio's abuse of him. To the Duke himself and the Senators he yields no more than the respect due to his

> very noble and approved good masters . . .

They shall hear his "round unvarnished tale"; he will call one witness, Desdemona; and upon her word—nor when she comes does he even first speak to her lest he seem to bias it—will he be judged.

By touch after touch Shakespeare builds up the figure, and upon its present calm and poise the lightest is effective. Since he was a very child—since his arms had "seven years' pith"—he has known only war and adventure. And, but for love of Desdemona, he would not now put his "unhoused free condition" into "circumscription and confine." War calling, they must both obey; he leaving her then and there, she following him into danger if she may. His austerity protests that it will not be

> To please the palate of my appetite . . .

her courage that it is even

> to his honours and his valiant parts . . .

that she has consecrated "soul and fortunes." It is no ordinary marriage. There is nothing commonplace in either of them.

There is little tenderness in their parting:

> Come, Desdemona; I have but an hour
> Of love, of worldly matters and direction,
> To spend with thee. . . .

—that is all. But she accepts it so, the soldier's wife already. It is only after their separation, when he finds her safe in Cyprus, preserved from the dangers of war and shipwreck, that he realizes how much she and this new and strange thing happiness mean to him.[69] He is awed—

> If it were now to die,
> 'Twere now to be most happy; for, I fear,
> My soul hath her content so absolute,
> That not another comfort like to this
> Succeeds in unknown fate.

69 Dangers more present to the Elizabethan mind—the minds of the play's first audience—than to our own. Yet in January 1940, as I write, this is hardly so.

—and amused—

O, my sweet,
I prattle out of fashion, and I dote
In mine own comforts.

by its hold on him. But he is as strict in discipline with himself as with others. It is his wedding night, but his parting orders to Cassio are:

to-morrow with your earliest
Let me have speech with you.

Unhappily for Cassio, he finds cause to speak with him still earlier. When the noise of the unpardonable broil has been quelled; quietly, sternly, curtly it is:

Cassio, I love thee;
But never more be officer of mine.

For in judgment he is swift and uncompromising. This is the last capital touch given to the picture of a still unscathed Othello. In retrospect we may recognize the danger that lay in a too inflexible perfection of poise; once upset, hard to regain.

It is the picture of a quite exceptional man; in high repute and conscious of his worth, yet not self-conscious; of a dignity which simplicity does not jeopardize; generous in praise of those who serve him; commanding respect without fear; frank and unsuspicious and ready to reciprocate affection. Yet he has been a man apart, alone. He is not young, has fought and adventured the world over, striking root nowhere. And he is black. The Venetians, truly, not only value his soldiership, but Brabantio, he says:

loved me, oft invited me . . .

They seemed to be treating him in everything as one of themselves. But to have him marry Desdemona! That would be quite another question. Neither he nor she was of the eloping kind; evidently no other way looked open to them. Lay a part of Brabantio's anger to the elopement itself, of the Duke's appeasing attitude to his wish, with the Turks attacking Cyprus, not to offend his only competent general. Yet that the daughter of a Venetian Senator should

to incur a general mock,
Run from her guardage to the sooty bosom . . .

—even of the renowned Othello—is conduct unnatural enough for her bewitching

> By spells and medicines bought of mountebanks . . .

to be a very likely way of accounting for it. Shakespeare does not need to spend much explanatory speech on all this. Othello's exotic figure and the contrast between the two will in themselves be eloquent of it. And should we, under the spell of his nobility, be inclined to forget it—since Desdemona could!—reminder will not be lacking. For Iago's defiling eye sees only this, reads only foulness and perversity into such enfranchisement.

But Desdemona

> saw Othello's visage in his mind . . .

That we may see him as she did the story of his life is repeated before the Senate and to us even as she heard it. And, says the Duke,

> I think this tale would win my daughter too.

It is in her fine faith in this vision of him that she goes forward, first to a happiness justifying and fulfilling it, then to its inexplicable shattering. He finds in happiness with her a self unrealized before. It is a self created by her love for him, and will be the more dependent, therefore, upon his faith in that. It will be, besides, a dangerously defenseless self, since he is no longer a young man when it comes to life in him, and between it and the rest of his character, fully formed and set in far other molds, there can be no easy interplay. This division between old and new in him—between seasoned soldier and enraptured bridegroom!—presages the terrible cleavage to come. He does not bring to his love for Desdemona, nor wish to, the measured wisdom which experience has taught him. It is against his judgment that he yields to her pleading for Cassio with a

> let him come when he will;
> I will deny thee nothing.

The romantic Cassio himself had acclaimed her as "our great captain's captain," of which Iago's acid version is that "our general's wife is now the general." He is, in fact—the elder husband, the young wife!—uxorious; yet less from weakness than in tribute to this miracle she has wrought in him. Could it prove illusion—he is at the height of happiness, challenging fate, Iago at his side—"chaos is come again." But even now, and for all their love, they see life differently. Adventure behind them, she has settled down to the workaday joys of a home, in which she can be confidently, merrily, carelessly herself, so confidently, we note, that his exasperation over the handkerchief gives her only passing concern. But he is still an uncharted stranger in this world, inapt, despite his quality, at its defense—which yet needs only the simple, natural instinct in a man, loving and so beloved, that all is well.[70]

Othello has a quick and powerful imagination. It is a gift which in a man of action may make either for greatness or disaster. It can be disciplined and refined into a perceptiveness, which will pierce to the heart of a problem while duller men are scratching its surface; it can divorce his mind from reality altogether. How is it that, even under stress, Othello does not unarguably perceive Desdemona's innocence and Iago's falsity? Instead his imagination only serves to inflame his passion. He is conscious of its unruliness.

> I swear 'tis better to be much abused
> Than but to know't a little.

—since imagination will multiply "little" beyond measure; that, when passion has dislodged reason in him, is his first cry. Imagination begets monstrous notions:

> I had been happy, if the general camp,
> Pioneers and all, had tasted her sweet body,
> So I had nothing known. . . .

And Iago keeps it fed with such kindred matter as the tale of Cassio's dream, with picturings increasingly physical, of her "naked with her friend a-bed," of Cassio's confessedly lying "with her, on her; what you will!"—until the explicit obscenity leaves imagination at a loss, and nature suspends the torment in

[70] Shakespeare shows us the two, upon the very edge of calamity, living together—as Cinthio tells us that his Moor and Desdemona were living—in "harmony and peace"; he contrives to insinuate thus much of this telling introduction to the story into the play.

the oblivion of a swoon. Later, self-torment takes the obscurer, perverser form of the "horrible fancy" which sees Desdemona as a whore in a brothel, himself among her purchasers; imagination run rabid.

But, in his right mind, he can be master of his imagination too. Call Iago an "artist in real life," if a spurious one; Othello is the poet born. While the soldier he is must hold to realities, the poet in him is free in a metaphysical world in which these find a rarer meaning. The tales that won Desdemona will have been of a poet's telling—anthropophagi and "men whose heads do grow beneath their shoulders" being mere curiosities in themselves—and the more roundly told and unvarnished the more befitting the matter and the man. We are still far from the Othello who hysterically charges a lost handkerchief with the very "mighty magic" he mocks at here.

From the beginning, when the occasion stirs him, the poet's mind shows. It shows in the delicate balance of idea and phrase, in the irony blended with beauty of

> Keep up your bright swords, for the dew will rust them.

It is a poet that seeks refuge from dishonor among imaged memories of a glory indefeasibly his, of

> the plumed troop and the big wars
> That make ambition virtue! . . .
> the neighing steed and the shrill trump,
> The spirit-stirring drum, the ear-piercing fife,
> The royal banner and all quality,
> Pride, pomp and circumstance of glorious war!

then to renounce them as a man renouncing life itself. This is not an exercise in rhetoric. The trumpet and drum, the fife and the banners, were themselves tokens of the metaphysical world, in which Othello found his life's meaning. The words are tokens too, which, in the melody and rhythm of the mounting phrases, he is setting to do all that words made musical may do to unveil that world for him again.

It is a world in which one lives alone. Iago—being what he is—has listened in amazed incomprehension. He will be ready, however, at its next unveiling, upon the black vision of

> the Pontic sea,
> Whose icy current and compulsive course
> Ne'er feels retiring ebb, but keeps due on
> To the Propontic and the Hellespont . . .

with a fine histrionic pretense to fellowship in it. Desdemona is given a horrifying glimpse of it as an anarchy of grotesque and infected images; flies quickening in the shambles, a winking moon, the bawdy wind—a world to which he brings the miseries bred in him. He reaches towards his metaphysical world once more in the rapt calm of

> It is the cause, it is the cause, my soul:
> Let me not name it to you, you chaste stars!
> It is the cause. . . .

to enter it, his murderous passion sated, and find it void:

> Methinks it should be now a huge eclipse
> Of sun and moon, and that the affrighted globe
> Should yawn at alteration.

—no lesser figure will serve.

Othello's, we said, is a story of blindness and folly, of a man run mad. As the play is planned, evil works all but unquestioned in him until it is too late. Of battle between good and evil, his soul the battleground, even of a clarifying consciousness of the evil at work in him, there is nothing. Not until the madman's deed is done, does "he that was Othello" wake to sanity again; his tragedy, then, to have proved that from the seemingly securest heights of his "soul's content" there is no depth of savagery to which man cannot fall. Yet, in face of the irrevocable deed savage and man are one.

Shakespeare paints us a merciless picture of the awakened, the broken Othello; of the frenetically repentant creature of Emilia's scornful

> Nay, lay thee down and roar. . . .

of the man with all strength for evil or for good gone out of him, remorse mere mockery as he looks upon the dead Desdemona; of an Othello crying

> Whip me, ye devils,
> From the possession of this heavenly sight!

> Blow me about in winds! roast me in sulphur!
> Wash me in steep-down gulfs of liquid fire! . . .

—sheer horror this; the howling of the damned! He speaks his own epitaph before he dies; a last echo of the noble Moor that was.

DESDEMONA, EMILIA, BIANCA

Desdemona's part in the play is a passive one. The single fateful step she takes has already been taken at the start. We have only to be told—and this we are told most explicitly—that she took it wholly of her own free will. Emilia, but for the sneaking of the handkerchief and one aimless explosion of wrath, remains passive until at last she unmasks Iago. Bianca is a cat's-paw. The economy of the action allows for no extraneous adventuring into the character of any of the three. They respond illuminatingly to its events; and by setting them in strong contrast each to the other Shakespeare makes them, all three, the more vivid. Desdemona and Bianca never even meet. But Cassio, turning so differently from the one to greet the other so cavalierly, links the two; and what Bianca is and what Desdemona—what in the face of Iago's slanders she so transparently is *not*—springs thus into higher relief. The three provide the play with something like a pattern of womankind—motherhood and old age omitted: Desdemona's fine nature set beside Emilia's coarseness, with the little trull Bianca, who

> by selling her desires
> Buys herself bread and clothes . . .

for their ape and counterfeit.

DESDEMONA

Desdemona appears in one scene only of the three which pass in Venice and speaks just twenty-seven lines. But the action and debate center on her, and when she has at last had her own say a very clear picture of her emerges.

What has happened is extraordinary enough in itself to rivet our attention. The tale of it is flung at us for a start in the crudest and most rancorous terms. Their rancor discounts them somewhat; still more does the sight of Othello himself, so evidently neither "gross" nor "lascivious," nor is he even found, as he might more suggestively be, in Desdemona's company. Brabantio's angry chatter about drugs, charms and witchcraft sounds overdone. But his talk of her as

> a maid so tender, fair and happy,
> So opposite to marriage that she shunned
> The wealthy curled darlings of our nation . . .

as

> A maiden never bold;
> Of spirit so still and quiet that her motion
> Blushed at herself . . .

has a likelier ring, and we expect explanation. Othello's may suffice the Duke, concerned for those Cyprus wars; but it takes Desdemona's own appearance fully to enlighten us. And the effect of it is unexpected. This "maiden never bold" is intimidated neither by her father nor "all this noble company." She does not turn to Othello for support, nor plead irresistible love for him, nor, indeed, offer any excuse whatever for her conduct. She speaks of duty, but as divided between past and future; once owed gratefully to her father, now, she challenges—there is defiance in the word!—due to her husband. Whatever else, here is no helpless maiden enticed away, whether by foul means or fair. Small wonder that, before such impassivity, Brabantio's distress freezes to a

> God be with you! I have done.

—after which, while he and the Duke exchange their neat, not too engrossing, "sentences," we can observe her mutely standing there. The war's threat to part her from Othello gives her speech again; as impassive in its admission of her father's final loss of her, but lucid and fervent—her heart bared without false shame—in the plea for her rights in the love for which she has dared so greatly. Again, here is a Desdemona unknown to her father, unknown, we may suppose, to Othello too, now stirring him for the first time from his soldier's restraint to an echo of her plea. But between the explicit calm with which she can speak her determined mind and this rare favor lies in her nature a reticent and inarticulate zone, unguarded, and to prove of mortal peril to her.

Brabantio's

She has deceived her father, and may thee.

—which Othello so trenchantly flings back at him, which Iago stores in his memory—is more false than true. He was deceived in her, as, with less excuse, Othello will be. She was to blame for letting him stay too long self-deceived. But there was he who should have known her best, knowing her so little as never even to suspect what ardor and resolve might lie beneath her accustomed quiet. Hard to confide in him in any case, all but impossibly hard to tell him that she loved the alien "black" Othello. How convince him but by doing as she did? It has taken the unexpected threat of separation to make her speak her heart out even now; but, speaking out, it is with no apology. Under vile accusation later on she will swear to her innocence. But if this and no more sounds better evidence of baser guilt—why, of explanations, arguments, self-justifyings, of any of the means of defense commonly used by those who might be guilty though they are not, she, who could not be guilty, is incapable. Even as Othello went unprotected against the poison of mistrust of her, so she gives never a thought to protection against—how should she expect it?—his mistrust. It is she, in truth, who does not wear her heart upon her sleeve; confessing that

I am not merry; but I do beguile
The thing I am, by seeming otherwise.

and thereupon, to deaden her fears for Othello's safety, even letting Cassio flirt with her a little. She is no precisian in candor. To smooth down that unwarranted commotion over the mislaid handkerchief she does slightly economize the facts. Moments of great joy may leave her at a loss. Upon their reuniting all her response to Othello's eloquent ecstasy is a sober

The heavens forbid
But that our loves and comforts should increase,
Even as our days do grow!

She does not try to find words to express her deepest feelings; they are lodged too deep in her, they are too real. That she can plead as fluently as frankly for Cassio should be one sign at least—were any needed—that no more than her kindness is engaged.

Moments of misery leave her dumbfounded too. Out of her clear sky of happiness it comes, with no more warning than the pother about the handkerchief; before all the world Othello strikes her. And she has nothing to say but

I have not deserved this.

Then, first dismissed as a servant might be, when later she is summoned to him again, she does not reproach him, nor even refer to the incredibly terrible thing. She cannot. She is as helpless, too, to draw reasons for his anguished passion from him as he to give them. And when at last, lashing her with "strumpet" and "whore," he leaves her and the alarmed Emilia asks her how she does, her answer is

Faith, half asleep.

She will not talk of what has passed even to Emilia. When she sends Iago to Othello to plead for her, she cannot bring herself to speak the word that has so shamed her.[71] Childish of her; but, as she says, she is "a child to chiding." Has she no pride, that she, Brabantio's daughter, who could face Duke and Senate with composure, is on her knees before Iago? But innocence has a dignity of its own, a courage too. When, at this instant, the trumpets sound to supper, she does not need his admonition to "go in and weep not" to embolden her to do her ceremonial duty with perfect calm. Supper done, and Lodovico having taken formal leave of her, she falls back again into an obedient humility.

But, alone with Emilia, the blow, and the worse blow of

that cunning whore of Venice
That married with Othello.

seem to have numbed her mind. One might suppose that she no longer cared even to learn of what she is accused. But it is largely sheer fatigue; and beneath the surface, where reality lies, she is as sensitively alive as ever, and to what is, for her, the

[71] It may well seem that Shakespeare has here stretched a psychological point in his wish to complete the pattern of Iago's triumph; first, Othello senseless at his feet and now Desdemona kneeling there. Would she have sent him to Othello? Such unlikelihood as there may be is lessened a little by the stress laid on the fact that he is Emilia's husband, she by this her mistress' friend. But one suspects that, as with the plainly imported meeting between blind Gloucester and mad Lear, it was the effectiveness of the pattern which counted.

essential thing. She is a great lady, and has been publicly insulted —and worse. She is innocent, and has been foully slandered. She is a Venetian, and has surely but to appeal to Lodovico and Venice to protect her from this alien, this Moor—against whom, how rashly, she would not be warned. But she makes no such move, advances no such claims. She holds still by the faith in his "very quality," for which she clairvoyantly came to love him. For better or worse he is now her lord; and to her

> even his stubbornness, his checks, his frowns . . .
> have grace and favour in them.

Nor will proper pride, nor just resentment with all the arguments in the world for aid, change that. Better pleading will be those emblems of her chastity, her wedding sheets—to the obtuse Emilia they are just "those sheets!"—laid tonight on their bed. And when the time comes, what fitter shroud! She is not conscious, as we are, that her death is near; only that, if sorrow cannot change her, nor will time. Emilia tries to rally her with a robust

> Come, come, you talk!

She finds expression for her "wretched fortune," not in its own bewailing, but in the melody which expressed poor Barbara's, and in that an anodyne. And so little does she anticipate calamity that, quitting her cryptic spiritual solitude, she can idly turn her thoughts to Lodovico, play the tolerant married lady with shrugging "O, these men, these men," and, in the sequent

> Dost thou in conscience think—tell me, Emilia—
> That there be women do abuse their husbands
> In such gross kind?

be suspected by Emilia of playing—and overplaying—the innocent too.

But Emilia hardly understands her here, nor she fully perhaps herself. If she is now to live a life deformed by jealousy and suspicions, it will not suffice her simply to be sure that she does not deserve them, would not

> do such a deed for all the world.

Self-complacency is cold comfort. But some habitation of faith she must have; so she will exchange the glory of her lost ideal for the companionable shelter of that gently obstinate delusion:

> I do not think there is any such woman.

But Desdemona's truth outshines such ingenuous streaks of self-deceptions, or the scared fib about the handkerchief, even as it transfigures the incredible lie of her dying answer to Emilia's

> O, who hath done this deed?

—the heart-rending

> Nobody; I myself. Farewell.
> Commend me to my kind lord. . . .

—into a shaming of the mere truth. Emilia finds the word:

> O, she was heavenly true!

—not simply true to Othello, but to herself and her faith in him. This is betrayed, and she is wantonly and savagely killed. No ray of light pierces there. But they could not kill her faith—in the Othello that remained to her, for her still the true Othello, and the beauty of this.

EMILIA

Emilia is coarse clay. She is of Shakespeare's own invention, no kin to the Ensign's wife in the story. He develops her—with the economy of his maturer stagecraft—by the measure of his need for her. An attractive young woman, from whom Cassio finds it good fun to claim a kiss, Iago's pretended fears for his "night-cap" being given that much color; such is our first impression of her. She stays mumchance enough for the moment to bear out Desdemona's bantering defense of her:

> Alas, she has no speech.

But—while what Iago may say is no evidence—she will later amply corroborate his

> In faith, too much!
> I find it still when I have list to sleep. . . .

by showing that she can chide very much more trenchantly than "with thinking" if she is stirred to it.

Shakespeare already has clearly in mind what he wants of her; and upon the

> I am glad I have found this napkin. . . .

and in the short exchange with Iago (their single scene alone together) he more definitely shapes her to it, and briskly, with the

> This was her first remembrance from the Moor:
> My wayward husband hath a hundred times
> Wooed me to steal it; but she so loves the token—
> For he conjured her she should ever keep it—
> That she reserves it evermore about her
> To kiss, and talk to. I'll have the work ta'en out,
> And give't Iago. What he will do with it
> Heaven knows, not I;
> I nothing but to please his fantasy.

Beside the neighboring subtleties of Iago's dealing with Othello the packed utility of this may seem technically a little crude. But Shakespeare will not interrupt that chief issue for long; and since there is little subtlety about Emilia, the artlessness of the soliloquy pictures her the better:

> My wayward husband . . .

—her incurious, tolerant, pedestrian mind finds this the aptest term for Iago's restless exigence and uncertain temper—

> hath a hundred times
> Wooed me to steal it . . .

—to which point she would not go, and will not, as she answers him, admit to be going now:

> No. faith; she let it drop by negligence,
> And, to the advantage, I being here took't up.

It is a nice distinction. But she that can make it will have the less difficulty in setting down her honest Iago's share in the business to "fantasy." Better to please him too, and to find herself his "good wench" for a change from his perpetual chiding (he greets her testily; her first words to him are "Do not you chide": these jolly fellows, such good company abroad, are often less so at home); and better, by far, she must have found, not to cross him or question him if his "wit" begins to turn "the seamy side without," as it does when, misgiving seizing her, she begs the handkerchief again. "'Tis proper I obey him" is her wifely code, and the mere tone of his present

> Be not acknown on't; I have use for it.
> Go, leave me.

must warn her that she will be wise to obey him pretty promptly in this. Yet she must be conscious too that there is mischief in the matter. What licit use could he have for the handkerchief? But she chooses to shut her mind and hold her tongue.

Having thus committed her to a peccadillo which she will be loath to avow he runs the less risk of her betraying him; and, in fact, the occasion soon arising, she lies smoothly and efficiently. It is before Othello's clamor over the loss that she does so. After this it is even less easy to recant and confess; nor could she without involving Iago and incurring his anger, since she no longer has the handkerchief to restore. But Desdemona's own fib about it seems, by comparison, to lighten hers; nor, apparently, is the handkerchief the real cause of the clamor, a pretext only for such a fit of truculent ill-temper as any wife must learn to expect from any husband. Once again, then, she shuts her mind.

Not that the diabolical truth could come at present within the range of her most vigilant suspicions. She does not think very highly of the masculine nature, nor express herself very delicately about it:

> 'Tis not a year or two shows us a man:
> They are all but stomachs and we all but food;
> They eat us hungerly, and when they are full
> They belch us.

But if lack of imagination leaves her blind to the heights it lets her ignore the blacker depths around her too. The Iago of the play's opening, envious and false beneath his honest surface, she will long enough have known for her husband; but of the demi-devil committed to Cassio's death and Desdemona's, and to Othello's ruin, how should she have an inkling?

While she herself, however, is hardened to jealousies and "chidings"—and of these can give as good as she gets—her lady, she soon sees, is not so thick-skinned; nor, she suspects, would Othello's jealousy, once roused, be likely to end in mere bluster. Hence her "Pray heaven" that "no conception nor no jealous toy" "possess him" and her "Lady, amen!"—graver by far than Desdemona's own conscience-free

> Heaven keep that monster from Othello's mind!

And her fears are soon justified. Then it is another facet of

Emilia that we see, standing stubbornly up to Othello in defense of a mistress she has learned to love, ready to stake her soul that

> if she be not honest, chaste and true,
> There's no man happy; the purest of their wives
> Is foul as slander.

He dismisses her. But she has not, we find later, been above listening at the door to the terrible invective thrown on Desdemona; and her loyal indignation rises the higher at it and its meek receiving, and the higher yet upon encountering Iago's disconcertingly tepid sympathy—and some instinct seems suddenly to set her on a trail:

> I will be hanged, if some eternal villain,
> Some busy and insinuating rogue,
> Some cogging, cozening slave, to get some office,
> Have not devised this slander. . . .

We are at one of the play's crucial moments, and it is upon Emilia—upon what she will now do, what fail to do—that the event turns. Iago's dry

> Fie, there's no such man; it is impossible.

is a plain caution to her to follow that trail no further. Later, rent by remorse, she will avow that "I thought so then," and the "then" is now. She has, of course, no reason to suppose Desdemona in mortal danger, she merely sees her suffering more keenly what other wives suffer; and if Iago is drawing some still hidden crooked profit from it, his tart

> Speak within door. . . .
> You are a fool; go to.

is yet plainer warning that the less she says or knows the better for her. So she satisfies her outraged feelings with a few high-sounding words, and for the third time, and this time fatally, she obediently shuts her mind. If her conscience is uneasy it will be lightened when she remarks, upon her next sight of Othello, that "he looks gentler than he did." And then she relaxes, despite misgivings, into her habitual matter-of-fact mood, administering to her wounded, delicate Desdemona a good-night dose, not of the compassion she feels, but of a cheerful toughening conjugal doctrine of give and take, prophylactic for the future.

To the shock of the murder upon this night of murders is added the poignancy of Desdemona's death in her own arms--by so little is she too late to save her! To this succeeds stupefaction:

O, who hath done this deed?
Nobody; I myself. . . .

and to that, under ban of the devoted, incredible lie, the moment's helplessness of

She said so: I must needs report the truth.

Then Othello's

She's like a liar gone to burning hell:
'Twas I that killed her.

sets her anguished wrath free to rage—until it is checked as by a blow at his

Thy husband knew it all.

For a stunned while she can only repeat and repeat

My husband ! . . My husband ! . .
My husband say that she was false?

—each answer the tearing of a screen from before that closed mind. Yet when Iago appears he must—he, her husband!—clear himself if he can, as surely he can. He does so, sufficiently:

I told him what I thought, and told no more
Than what he found himself was apt and true.

—and a woman of common sense might well leave it at that. Desdemona is dead. What is her good name worth? Emilia will not.

But did you ever tell him she was false?

He can hedge no further. Othello is listening. He faces her, this unsuspected Emilia, with a blunt "I did," and she brands him before them all as a liar.

But Desdemona's innocence so proclaimed and believed, might she not now at least "charm her tongue" and excusably let things go their way? Again she will not. There is worse hidden, and out it shall come, and she will purge herself too of her own share of the guilt—

I thought so then: I'll kill myself for grief. . . .

—of the guilt of the blind eye and closed mind. What this may cost her she has time to reckon while Othello lies there prostrate with remorse and Gratiano recites his mild elegy, clear warning of it in Iago's tensely vigilant silence; he has already bidden her be gone. She has only to hold her tongue as before about that tragically ridiculous handkerchief. Yet again she will not. The threatening sword is half-drawn; she might still save herself; she will not. She brings his crime home to him, confesses her ignorant share in it, and he kills her.

The coarse-grained, conscienceless, light-minded Emilia proves capable of this. She could love an Iago; she gives her life in testimony of the dead Desdemona's innocence. She passes from her merrily cynical

> Why, who would not make her husband a cuckold to make him a monarch? I should venture purgatory for't.

to a

> Moor, she was chaste; she loved thee, cruel Moor;
> So come my soul to bliss, as I speak true. . . .

Othello does not heed. She prays to be lifted to her mistress' side, but they let her lie where she has fallen. Her senses failing, she can only cry pitifully

> What did thy song bode, lady?
> Hark, canst thou hear me?

Desdemona can no longer hear. The memory of a melody, of that "Willow, willow, willow . . ." must serve for communion between them. But Emilia has won herself a place in the play's tragic heaven.

BIANCA

The little hussy Bianca is Desdemona's very opposite, and our first sight of her is meant to make this plain. For Cassio, taking respectful leave of the one in her gentleness and dignity, turns to find himself at once accosted by the pretty, flaunting impudence of the other—who actually is to him, moreover, what Iago, abusing Othello's ear, would have Desdemona to be. And the mocking, scurrilous talk of her which Othello, eavesdropping, overhears is made to seem talk of Desdemona.

Iago, as his nature is, speaks brutally of her and to her; of her "selling her desires," addresses her, when he wants to implicate her in the midnight ambush laid for Cassio, as a "notable strumpet," and wags a moral head over such "fruits of whoring." But it is the respectable Emilia's gratuitously added

> Fie, fie upon thee, strumpet!

which touches the young woman on the raw, and evokes the shrilly protesting

> I am no strumpet; but of life as honest
> As you that thus abuse me.

She is, of course, a trull, no better, and ill-behaved at that. She pursues her lover in the streets, makes scenes there, flies into tantrums, turns as jealous as her betters. The gallant Cassio, more than a little vain of her infatuation for him, treats her as such creatures must expect to be treated. But she is shrewd and witty. To the gallant cant of Cassio's

> Not that I love you not.

she retorts with a neat

> But that you do not love me.

She is plucky; she stands up to Iago's bullying. She may even love her lover in her disreputable way. For Shakespeare she is at least a human being.

BRABANTIO, CASSIO, RODERIGO

BRABANTIO

Brabantio is redeemed from the convention of the hoodwinked father by a few specific strokes. He swings between extremes, from his high regard for Othello to insensate abuse of him, through a chill pardon for Desdemona, in which past tenderness still echoes, to the cutting farewell:

> She has deceived her father, and may thee.

He seems exceptionally credulous about

> spells and medicines bought of mountebanks . . .

but he takes a detached view of his own nature, "glad at soul" that he has no other child, since Desdemona's escape would teach him "tyranny, to hang clogs on them." He passes from a frantic bustle of pursuit:

> Raise all my kindred. . . .
> Call up my brother. . . .
> Some one way, some another. . . .
> At every house I'll call. . . .

to quiet, solitary dignity before the Senate, as from clamor for vengeance on Othello to the magnanimous

> If she confess that she was half the wooer,
> Destruction on my head, if my bad blame
> Light on the man!

And then and there, despite grief and defeat, he is capable of capping the Duke's encouraging platitudes with some very smooth irony. But it looks as if the shock and the strain may have broken him, and when he speaks of his "bruised heart" he means it. And later we hear that Desdemona's loss

> was mortal to him, and pure grief
> Shore his old thread in twain.

CASSIO

The Folio's list of characters calls Cassio *an Honourable Lieutenant*. He is seemingly a man of gentle birth, and of education; Iago mocking at his "bookish theoric." He is the unwitting implement of evil, its stalking-horse, and his place in the play's scheme is that of an average, unheroic, well-meaning man caught between tragic extremes—of wickedness and of the nobility it betrays. His faults are failings, redeemable by his own recognition of them. But here he sways, haplessly, somewhat ridiculously, between extremes within himself. He knows that he has "very poor and unhappy brains for drinking," yet he yields from good nature to the claims of good fellowship, though he says, even as he does so, "it dislikes me." He is sensitive even to self-consciousness, and, beyond that, to the point of self-display. Having listened in disciplined silence to Othello's sentence on him, in his heartfelt outburst to Iago, the

> Reputation, reputation, reputation. O, I have lost my reputation! I have lost the immortal part of myself, and what remains is bestial. My reputation, Iago, my reputation!

we remark that he is listening, not unappreciatively, to the sounds of his own despair. Such misery does not strike deep, nor last long; its enjoyment is soon exhausted. Iago tactfully gives it scope, and Cassio, disburdened, not only accepts his optimistic advice without question, but will "betimes in the morning . . . beseech the virtuous Desdemona" to plead his cause.[72] For may not Othello's anger dissolve as easily—so this mood bids him hope—as has the bitterness of his own remorse? The man is mercurial. He is a lightweight. But there is with that something boyish about him, and appealing. Despite his despair, he thinks to bring musicians to play the customary nuptial *aubade* beneath Othello's windows; an ingenuous piece of propitiation.

He is a romantic soul. We have him, during those first moments in Cyprus, rhapsodizing over "the divine Desdemona." He is gaily gallant, finds it good fun to claim a kiss of welcome from Emilia. And Iago's "profane and liberal wit" having served its purpose while they all wait anxiously for news of Othello, he takes his turn at distracting Desdemona, more delicately and intimately, yet openly and respectfully, galling Iago with envy of his address in "such tricks," in kissing his "three fingers" and playing "the sir," having already—how thoughtlessly—patronizingly disparaged his Ancient's good breeding to her, with that

> He speaks home, madam: you may relish him more in the soldier than in the scholar.

But he has a finer sense than all this shows of Desdemona's quality. She is for him—the epithet springs spontaneously—"the virtuous Desdemona." Nor will he join in the accepted marriage pleasantries, meets Iago's ribald

> Our general . . . hath not yet made wanton the night with her, and she is sport for Jove.

with a cold snub. And her "bounteous" compassion on him when he is in trouble raises respect to very reverence.

His attitude towards Bianca is of a piece with the rest of him. She is his mistress, she is "a customer," and he scoffs merrily at "the monkey's" pretense that he means to marry her. But he

[72] Note how Cassio's impulsiveness helps give the needed speed to the action.

treats her, even as Shakespeare does, decently and humanely. He does not care to have her pursue him in the street—who would? —and, being what she is, she must put up with a blunt

> leave me for this time. . . .
> I do attend here on the general;
> And think it no addition, nor my wish
> To have him see me womaned.

nor does he scruple to round on her pretty sharply when she vexes him. But, this apart, she is his "most fair Bianca," his "sweet love." He excuses himself with courteous insincerity for a week's neglect of her, protesting that he loves her, paying her in that coin too. He is a gentleman, and she, as the phrase goes, is no better than she should be. But he would never be guilty, to her face or behind her back, of the grossness of Iago's "This is the fruits of whoring."

The weakness which lets him drink when he knows he cannot carry his liquor is matched by his broken resolve to break with Bianca. He has kept it for a week; and, confiding to Iago what an infatuated nuisance she is, he protests:

> Well, I must leave her company.

Yet a moment later, after she has told him in a fit of tantrums to come and sup with her that same night or see her no more, Iago dryly demanding if he means to, he answers shruggingly:

> Faith, I intend so.

the full truth being, it would seem, that he is both secretly flattered by her scandalous infatuation for him—he makes the most of it:

> She falls me thus about my neck. . . . So hangs and lolls and weeps upon me; so hales and pulls me. . . .

—and not a little afraid of her. It is at this point in the play that he, with Othello, is brought to the lowest pitch of indignity; puppets the two of them in Iago's hands, the one turned eaves-dropper, the other fatuously vaunting his conquest of a light-o'-love.

But a worthier finish is reserved him. For his would-be murder he utters no harsher reproach than

> Dear general, I never gave you cause.

and his epitaph upon Othello is fitly felt:

For he was great of heart.

And—though here, if the story were to have a sequel, we might question Senatorial judgment—he is left to rule in Cyprus.

RODERIGO

The Folio is as exact with its "Roderigo, *a gull'd Gentleman*"; but to this stock figure also Shakespeare gives human substance. It tells another tale of moral degradation; Iago the unresisted instrument. For Roderigo begins as an honorable suitor for Desdemona's hand; and, for his service in sounding the alarm, he converts Brabantio straightway from the

In honest plainness thou hast heard me say
My daughter is not for thee. . . .

to a

good Roderigo, I'll deserve your pains.

And what could be more correct than the long, elaborate, pedantically parenthetical address to the newly wakened and distracted father at the window, with which he justifies his interference?

I beseech you,
If't be your pleasure and most wise consent,
As partly I find it is . . .

—a mild effort at sarcasm—

that your fair daughter,
At this odd-even and dull watch of the night,
Transported with no worse nor better guard
But with a knave of common hire, a gondolier . . .

—as who might say today: carried off in a taxi-cab, not even a private car!—

To the gross clasps of a lascivious Moor—
If this be known to you, and your allowance . . .

—sarcasm again!—

We then have done you bold and saucy wrongs;
But if you know not this, my manners tell me
We have your wrong rebuke. . . .

—a neat antithesis!—

Do not believe,
That, from the sense of all civility,
I thus would play the trifle with your reverence:
Your daughter, if you have not given her leave . . .

—he fancies his sarcasm—

I say again, hath made a gross revolt,
Tying her duty, beauty, wit and fortunes,
In an extravagant and wheeling stranger . . .

—his vocabulary too!—

Of here and everywhere. . . .

—and could listen to his own eloquence all night. We see Iago in the background, a-grin at the foolish exhibition.

Roderigo's renewed hopes soar high, then, as he sticks by the grateful Brabantio and follows him to the Senate, but only to collapse again utterly upon the surrendering of Desdemona to Othello. He stands there mute, would be left alone and ignored even by Iago, did he not at last utter a plaintive

What will I do, thinkest thou? . . .
I will incontinently drown myself.

—the "silly gentleman" at his silliest, most pitiable, least unlikable.

He goes to the devil with his eyes open, yet blindly. His poor mind is no better than a sounding board for Iago's sophistries. Yet he takes each step downward most advisedly, and even in admitting his folly he persists in it. He is an incorrigible fool. To put money—for Iago—in his purse, to follow the wars—and Desdemona—he will sell all his land, uproot and leave himself to the mercy of events.[73] And his moral sense is as feeble and obscure as his mind is muddled. Since he cannot win Desdemona for his wife, he may get her—Iago persuades him—as a mistress, may cuckold Othello. There will be manly satisfaction in that. But when he hears that she is in love with Cassio:

Why, 'tis not possible. . . . I cannot believe that in her; she's full of most blessed condition.

[73] This final flourish to his scene with Iago:

I am changed: I'll go sell all my land.

had a significance for Shakespeare's audience that it cannot have for us.

And it is not, seemingly, that he thinks his own charms, given their chance, would make way with her, for he listens, unprotesting, to their most unflattering comparison with Cassio's. A less convinced, a more unconvincing, libertine there could hardly be. Finally, however, patience and cash exhausted, he protests, and, in a prepared oration, following the one he launched at Brabantio's window, he calls Iago to account. He has been let in—such is the tone of it—for a pretty poor investment, financially and morally too, and must now save what he can from the wreck:

> The jewels you have had from me to deliver to Desdemona would half have corrupted a votarist: you have told me she hath received them and returned me expectations and comforts of sudden respect and acquaintance; but I find none. . . . I will make myself known to Desdemona. If she will return me my jewels, I will give over my suit and repent my unlawful solicitation; if not, assure yourself I will seek satisfaction of you.

Is there, after all, any real vice in the creature? He sees himself handed back his jewels while he makes Desdemona yet another carefully prepared little speech of polite regret for ever having dreamed of committing adultery with her. And his amorous advances, we may suspect, would have been hardly more formidable.

But if there is no passion in him, evil or good, to stimulate, such little mind as he possesses Iago does most successfully corrupt. The denigration of Desdemona is left to sink in; the less he believes in her virtue, the readier he will be to continue his pursuit of her; his final complaint is that the jewels have had no effect. The "satisfying reasons" he has received for Cassio's death we do not hear; but an echo of them can be caught in the callous

> 'Tis but a man gone.

with which, craven in his ambush, he draws a clumsy sword. With Iago for guide, he has traveled from the lovelorn folly of

> I will incontinently drown myself.

to this. Even so, he is no more of a success as a murderer than he has been as an adulterer; and his bravo's

> Villain, thou diest!

is promptly changed, with Cassio's sword between his own ribs instead, into an abjectly repentant

O, villain that I am!

A last disillusion is due; his mentor's face mockingly grinning, his friend's dagger stuck in him—

O damned Iago; O inhuman dog!

Disillusion indeed! But he is so futile a fool that we spare him some pity.

The Verse

OUT of an inheritance, in the main of blank verse and the ten-syllable couplet, but with the octo-syllabic and even the "old fourteener" never quite forgotten, and with a generous place left for prose, Shakespeare develops the dramatic speech of his art's maturity. He makes it an instrument which is both supple and powerful and of a wide range of effect, sensitive to the interpreting of thought charged with emotion, and allowing a sufficiently seeming spontaneity of expression without loss of coherent form. *Julius Cæsar*, with its virile chorus of conspirators, Cassius' passion, Brutus' calm and Antony's adroit modulations from mood to mood, may be said to see him master of the means to it. Then comes *Hamlet*, with Hamlet himself to give it greater freedom and a new intensity.

For with *Hamlet* Shakespeare breaks bounds, to enter and make his own—and no one has followed him there—a land of rarer and harder drama altogether. The dominant figures of the great post-*Hamlet* plays live and move in a larger imaginative area. Lear scales heights as Macbeth descends to deeps without precedent. The Antony brought to bay at Actium stands a giant, a "triple pillar of the world" indeed, beside the clever fellow who outplayed Brutus and Cassius. And Shakespeare has need of more powerful and resourceful means of expression still.

Of any revolution in his stagecraft there could be little question. Though the theater for which he has learned to work is grown richer, its mechanical and pictorial aspects remain fundamentally and unaccommodatingly the same. Nor has he ever made much of its shows and tricks, such as they are. His plays depend upon more essential things.

He might have followed Jonson's precepts and practice—who would, incidentally (some later critics to prove heartily in accord), have counseled him to leave such a subject as that of *King Lear* alone—and have entrenched himself in a strict formula, within which expression gains even an intenser power because it cannot expand. But one does not see him bartering freedom for security. It had not become him, as an aspiring "shake-scene," and a mere theater hack, to dwell upon theory and rule. It was for him to turn to account any convention whatever that might suit a particular occasion. And having learned all "the tricks of the trade," he will not, in these days of his mastership, discard from his store a single one of them. The Chorus, the Presenters, the Dumb Show, a Prologue or an Epilogue—devices not to be depended on, but there may be fitness and utility in them still. A Chorus proves but an encumbrance to the swift movement of *Romeo and Juliet*, and is rejected, seemingly in midcourse; but he can turn one to good use as a courier for the heavily equipped *Henry V*, and as the best and simplest means by which to "slide o'er sixteen years" in *The Winter's Tale*. The first part of *Henry IV* asks, to his thinking, no prologue; but "Rumour, painted full of tongues" makes a useful mnemonic link with the second. Rosalind's epilogue pays overt homage to convention; its dramatic use is to reconcile the comedy itself with the concluding masque. A dumb show would go ill indeed with the intense actualities of *Hamlet*; it is quite in place in *The Murder of Gonzago*, and markedly distinguishes the play within the play from the play. And even presenters, let vanish from the early *Taming of the Shrew*, make a short and qualified reappearance—as if to acknowledge the play's sophistication—in *Cymbeline*.[74] So too with his verse. He soon shook free of cramping or unmanageable meters and overelaborate artifice, strung-out alliteration, classical tags, multiple puns and the like. But with his art at its ripest, his verse at its freest, he still does not forbid himself a neat little passage

[74] The episode of the apparitions and Jupiter's descent has, I know, been labeled spurious. But, in its main lines at least, it may, I think, be called Shakespeare's, and with the more likelihood, perhaps, if this aspect of it is considered.

of stychomythia in *Antony and Cleopatra*, a few octosyllabics in *Measure for Measure*; and in *King Lear*, as a fitting auxiliary to Lear's madness, we have a very medley of vernacular song, mime and antic.

From *Othello* we can pick in this category, the Clown, the Duke's "sentences" and Iago's extempore rhyming.[75] Shakespeare has fitting use for each. As to the first; the strain of the play's action is continuous and at times intense, and the identifiable characters are all caught into its rapidly flowing main stream. The strain upon an audience will, moreover, be greater if, in performance, there are no marked intervals between acts and scenes. The anonymous Clown with his conventional jokes (coarse for the minstrels, innocuous for Desdemona) is the only completely contrasted "relief" afforded us. And it is to be noted that, of his two appearances, one occurs when our attention has been closely held by Iago throughout the long scene of the night of Cassio's downfall and just before the yet longer passage, in which Othello travels the entire distance from cloudless happiness to the savage dooming of Desdemona to death (a passage in which concentration and strain will be at their closest and tensest) and the other just after this.

The Duke's sententious "sentences" make on us and in the scene the effect they fail to make more directly on Brabantio, of "a grise or step" between the concluded turmoil of the elopement and the ardor for the coming departure to Cyprus and the wars. The Duke pronounces them from his chair of state as an informal and kindly judgment upon the case brought before him; the artifice of their form befits this, their smooth cadence the emollient content, while the couplets sound a full close. And Brabantio's ironically echoing reply—respectful, acquiescent; but he is as good at "sentences" as the Duke!—provides him with a dignified and effective retreat from the action. Shakespeare wants, without any too sudden change in the steering, without upsetting its balance, to set his scene upon another course; and this is as legitimate a way as any other.

Iago's six couplets of impromptu rhyming are semi-comic relief

[75] It would be pedantry to add the Herald; the convention of his speech will pass unobserved upon any nonrealistic stage.

to the strain—not on the audience, but on Desdemona while she waits for news of Othello's safety. Therefore they can be fully "dramatized"; the accomplishment, such as it is, being accounted an item in Iago's equipment, and well it becomes his intellectual swagger.

Utility is Shakespeare's sole test. He will employ any sort of device, however old and worn, if he can make it dramatically useful. The cumulative effect of the iteration of some single significant word; he has inherited this as a formula habitually carried to mechanical extremes. He never abandons it, only reduces it to the point at which it colorably reunites with our natural habit, upon which supposedly it was built, of recurring again and again under the stress of suffering, to the one thought that dominates our trouble. In *Othello* under various forms he makes frequent use of the device; directly, but within the limits of the spontaneous; oftener by inserting the iteration into the main body of speech; sometimes by using the significant word as "honest" and "honesty" are used—by the play's end what changes in tone and color, application and implication, have not been rung upon Iago's selected epithet![76]

The first noticeable bout of iteration is Cassio's in his lament for his lost reputation; and the sextuple repetition—though it is partly blended into his speech—gives the needed, in this case slightly comic, turn to his exaggerated grief. It can be matched and contrasted with Othello's tragic outcry when he suddenly wakes to the meaning of his terrible deed:

> If she come in, she'll sure speak to my wife;
> My wife! my wife! what wife? I have no wife.

and with Emilia's whelming

> Villainy, villainy, villainy!
> I think upon't: I think: I smell't: O villainy! . . .
> O villainy, villainy!

[76] It is Iago, speaking to Roderigo, who first employs the word for the "honest knaves" who are loyal to their masters. It is Othello who first attaches it to him with the

> So please your Grace, my Ancient;
> A man he is of honesty and trust. . . .

The epithet then sticks, with Iago himself acutely and angrily conscious of it.

Then there is the more complex, and so it will seem intentional

> Ay; you did wish that I would make her turn:
> Sir, she can turn, and turn, and yet go on,
> And turn again; and she can weep, sir, weep;
> And she's obedient, as you say, obedient,
> Very obedient. . . .

And since it habitually serves for the underscoring of some excess of emotion we shall in consequence find the device put oftenest to Othello's own use. It shapes his very first passionate outpouring; the

> O, now for ever
> Farewell the tranquil mind! farewell content!
> Farewell the plumed troop and the big wars
> That make ambition virtue! O, farewell!
> Farewell the neighing steed and the shrill trump . . .
> Farewell! Othello's occupation gone!

And, after this, instance upon instance of its employment can be found; the iterated word being either woven into a speech, when it not only heightens but controls the emotion, as with the

> It is the cause, it is the cause, my soul: . . .
> It is the cause. . . .

and with

> Put out the light, and then put out the light. . . .

—the word and idea, to be thrice more repeated, binding this section of the speech together as does a recurring note a passage in music—or it may be given the simple cumulative emphasis of

> O, blood, blood, blood! . . .
> O, fool, fool, fool! . . .

Finally, we have iteration turned to a far-related use; a word and the idea distributed over the greater part of a scene, and recurring later; played upon with varying intonations and implications, as Iago plays upon "think" and "thoughts," "jealousy" and "honesty," until he has Othello repeating them too and letting them have their way—Iago's way—with him.

But Shakespeare's verse is the master-medium of his stagecraft; and to make it the comprehensive means of expression which it now is, and which he operates with such freedom and ease, he has absorbed into it—and will often transform until they are hardly to be recognized—not a few conventions and forms. Take the verse of any scene in the play, and try to determine its normal measure. The ten-syllable, five-beat line is still there, if not manifestly, then—and more often—embedded in the dominant rhythm. But the speaker—and it is a question of speech—who sets to work upon a finger-tapping basis of rule and exception, with account to be taken of the use of extra syllables, of the curtailed or overrun line, of weak endings and the like, will soon find himself at a feeble and tangled halt. Let him rather acquire an articulate tongue, an unfailing ear for the pervasive melody and cadence of the verse, let him yield to its impetus, and—provided, of course, that he knows more or less what it is all about, and this sympathetic self-surrender will aid him there—Shakespeare can be counted on to carry him through.

Not that the verse, freely and variously though it may flow, escapes into any excessive metrical latitude, such as, in later post-Shakespearian days, will bring the weapon that it is, meant to command attention, to breaking from simple weakness in the actors' hands. There is never the lack of a stiff short line for the forcible punctuating of any overambulatory passage, nor of a few successive lines of strict scansion to restore, for just so long, an exemplary discipline; or the border can be crossed into a stretch of the contrasted discipline of prose. For if Shakespeare will not barter freedom for sheer strength, neither will he sacrifice strength to freedom; and a play demands some overriding unity of treatment, some force which will bind it together, if it be only to counterbalance the naturally disintegrating tendency of the individualities and diverse methods of its actors. Variety must not be let deteriorate into patchwork.

The enriched vocabulary, the bolder syntax, the unconfined rhythm, those are the more patent attributes of the maturer verse; its intrinsic virtue lies in the ready power, now developed in it, to paint and reveal character—he turns his freedom to that use. The verse of a play may be shaped and colored as a whole by the nature of its subject and setting, as, very notably, is the verse of *Coriolanus*; or—another means to a like end—it may be in large part keyed to the interpreting of the play's central figure;

and the rest within range, demands of character and the action allowed for, will be responsive. The dominant influence upon the verse of *Othello* is Othello himself. At his appearance he sets it a tone very much—and appropriately—as an officer commanding can give a tone to his regiment. The "round unvarnished tale" is exemplary: speech that moves forward to a steady rhythm; the epithetic picked and significant, yet never in sound or sense overweighting the verse and retarding it; the imagery sparse, nor ever merely decorative, but bred always of the matter in hand and the moment's imagination. And if Cassio and Iago (on duty) and, later, Montano seem spontaneously to pattern their speech upon his, there is truth to character in that; and Desdemona, before the Senate, Othello beside her, will be, after her own fashion, as naturally responsive.

It is, so to say, upon another plane that the Duke and Senators respond in their kind. As characters they are not sharply individualized; there is nothing in them to combat such domination. This is so too with Lodovico, appearing towards the play's end as a figure of importance to the action, but of no more specific character than is indicated by the dignity of his mission, Desdemona's

This Lodovico is a proper man.

and Emilia's gayer hint. Gratiano is in the same category. But by now a mold for the run of the verse has been formed, and the speech—no demands of character or action to the contrary—tends to flow into it. The Othello influence is neither exact or constraining. It initiates a tone and rhythm, and some measure in the use of imagery, and, on those within his immediate reach, will inevitably be strong. But it allows ample scope for individual expression; Desdemona's, in character attuned to his; Emilia's, late awakened to the matching of his anger with her own.

The opposing factor is Iago—the Iago of the soliloquies and of the unguarded scenes with Roderigo. His speech at the play's opening—its impetus and forceful rhythm and lack of all melody, regular and irregular lines chasing and ousting one another—is eloquent of this first aspect of him, of his greedy malice, the itch of his envy. In the very vowels and the dry distastefully reiterated consonants of "be-lee'd . . . calmed . . . debitor . . . creditor . . . counter-caster" sounds his contempt for Cassio:

> But he, sir, had the election;
> And I . . .
> must be be-lee'd and calmed
> By debitor and creditor: thus counter-caster,
> He, in good time, must his lieutenant be. . . .

His pretentious cleverness is painted thick for the start of his first lesson to Roderigo:

> Our bodies are our gardens; to the which our wills are gardeners: so that if we will plant nettles or sow lettuce, set hyssop and weed up thyme, supply it with one gender of herbs, or distract it with many, either to have it sterile with idleness or manured with industry, why, the power and corrigible authority of this lies in our wills. . . .

—and so on. It impresses Roderigo. And from out the verbiage, the talk of "carnal stings" and "unbitted lusts," of which love, he takes it, is "a sect or scion," its satisfaction now "as luscious as locusts" to be "shortly as bitter as coloquintida," there does at last emerge an admirably plain "Put money in thy purse."

Roderigo's lessons in worldly wisdom are mostly framed to this pattern, and in prose, the best medium in which to call a spade a spade. Only once, when he is bewailing Cassio's cudgeling, does Iago hearten him with the swing and color of verse:

> Does't not go well? Cassio hath beaten thee,
> And thou by that small hurt hast cashiered Cassio:
> Though other things grow fair against the sun,
> Yet fruits that blossom first will first be ripe. . . .

—the melody as efficacious as the argument!

Iago's soliloquies are in verse. That befits their impulsive confidence. But there is little or none of the imaginative stuff of poetry in them; and this noticeable incongruity is as befitting.

He can always, when he chooses, suit both the matter and manner of his speech to the occasion and his company; "honest Iago" is to be seen, actorlike, under any aspect demanded. And, at grips with Othello, so supplely and swiftly does he shift his address, giving and taking, advancing and yielding, now deforming Othello's thoughts, now shaping his own to their shape, that

Iago the actor would seem to be, as the phrase goes, "lost in his part." But in that capacity lies his talent; and behind it there *is*, indeed, no Iago, only a poisoned and poisonous ganglion of cravings after evil.

The expressive range of the play's verse with its auxiliary prose is in its entirety a wide one. There are the utilitarian units of the messengers and the Herald who speak after their kind; there is the conventional Clown who speaks and acts after his; and the First, Second, Third and Fourth Gentlemen paint us the storm and the landfall as, it is recognized, such things may effectively be painted, this being the aim and end of their existence. Then, beneath its exotic setting and warlike trimmings, the play is, at its core, a "domestic tragedy"—and Shakespeare's only essay in this kind. So in the more familiar scenes the verse falls readily into a semblance of the to-and-fro of habitual talk. But, dominating all, is the heroic figure of Othello himself, built to an heroic scale of expression and able to animate the noblest poetic form.

The gamut must run, with no incongruous gap appearing, between the squabble over the handkerchief—

> Is't lost? is't gone? speak, is it out o' the way?
> Heaven bless us!
>   Say you?
> It is not lost; but what an if it were?
> How!
> I say it is not lost.
>   Fetch't, let me see it.
> Why, so I can, sir, but I will not now. . . .

—up to the highest pitch of imaginative emotion. The unity of the action makes of itself for unity of treatment, and its sustained tension will not let even the most loosely woven verse be altogether slackened. In the stress of his suffering the firm athletic temper of Othello's speech breaks; but through this it is to a natural and characteristic superlative that he lifts it in such a passage as

>   Like to the Pontic sea,
> Whose icy current and compulsive course
> Ne'er feels retiring ebb, but keeps due on
> To the Propontic and the Hellespont . . .

Nor, in its setting and at its moment, will the sacrificial

> It is the cause, it is the cause. . . .

seem hollow magniloquence beside the simple factual horror of Desdemona's murder; nor, after this, the tremendous

> Methinks it should be now a huge eclipse
> Of sun and moon. . . .

nor the dazzling

> Nay, had she been true,
> If heaven would make me such another world
> Of one entire and perfect chrysolite,
> I'ld not have sold her for it.

reduce Emilia by comparison to commonplace. The scene's charge of tragic emotion is enough for the fusing of whatever the range of its means of expression.

As he returns to sanity so Othello returns also to the old sober, lofty equilibrium of thought and speech. We have it in that

> Here is my journey's end, here is my butt
> And very sea-mark of my utmost sail. . . .

with its memory of "the sea's worth" which could be no more to him than the worth of Desdemona's love, of the storm which spared them for the calm joy of their reuniting, of the icy current of the Pontic sea which imaged to him his implacable revenge. And in his valediction, with the remoter memories of Aleppo and the Arabian trees, the

> then must you speak
> Of one that loved not wisely but too well;
> Of one not easily jealous, but, being wrought,
> Perplexed in the extreme . . .

we have it brought to simplicity itself, and the beauty of that.

NOTE A

OTHELLO'S COLOR

"Haply for I am black . . ."; it is Othello himself who says so. Certainly the word then and later was given wide range in such connection; it could be used to denote dark hair and complexion merely. But in this case the meaning is surely plain: he is a black man, not a white one. Roderigo's "thick-lips" on the other hand is simply abusive; and no actor of Othello is called upon to make himself repulsive to his audience—although, as to this, taste will vary both with time and clime. The dramatic point of the matter lies in Desdemona's

> I saw Othello's visage in his mind. . . .

and all that it conveys of the quality of her love for him, its courage and clairvoyance. His looks at least must stress this, not minimize it.

NOTE B

OTHELLO'S CHRISTIANITY

Shakespeare could not, of course, make much of this if he would, since religion was a subject forbidden to the theater; but the references to it are more than casual. It is implied in Brabantio's "Are they married, think you?" and in Iago's quickly sequent question to Othello: "Are you fast married?" Othello's appeal to the rioters is:

> For Christian shame, put by this barbarous brawl. . . .

And in Iago's next soliloquy he speculates upon the ease with which Desdemona could

> win the Moor, were't to renounce his baptism,
> All seals and symbols of redeemed sin . . .

The "sacred vow" by "yond marble heaven" may or may not be intended to indicate a backsliding towards his "paynim" past —I doubt if an average audience would seize the point. But the tragic irony of his command to her to say her prayers and be reconciled to Heaven before, in her innocence, he murders her, is patent, and could have been made more so by the stronger stressing of his conversion to Christianity. And his final likening of himself to the "circumcised dog" whom he smote in Aleppo once for beating a Venetian and traducing the state, just such a one as in his own person he smites now—here the reference to his Christianity and his betrayal of it is unmistakable, even though Shakespeare would not risk making it more definite.